THE LOGOS-STRUCTURE
OF THE WORLD

The reality of things is their light.

THOMAS AQUINAS
Commentary to *Liber de causis* 1, 6

GEORG KÜHLEWIND

THE LOGOS-STRUCTURE
OF THE WORLD

Language as Model of Reality

Translated by
Friedemann-Eckart Schwarzkopf

Translation edited and revised by Michael Lipson,
Sabine Seiler, and Christopher Bamford

Lindisfarne Press

In the same series:

The Cosmologist's Second:
The Riddle of Time in Theories of the Universe
Konrad Rudnicki

Matter and Mind:
Imaginative Participation in Science
Stephen Edelglass, Georg Maier,
Hans Gebert, John Davy

This book is a translation of *Die Logosstruktur der Welt: Sprache als Modell der Wirklichkeit*, published by Verlag Freies Geistesleben, Stuttgart, Germany, in 1986.

Translation © G. Kühlewind and F. Schwarzkopf, 1986.
Peaceful Valley Farm, 20465 Placer Hills Road
Colfax, California 95713 U.S.A.

Published by Lindisfarne Press
RR 4, Box 94 A1, Hudson, NY 12534

Library of Congress Cataloging-in-Publication Data

Kühlewind, Georg.
    [Logosstruktur der Welt. English]
    The logos-structure of the world: language as model of reality
    / Georg Kühlewind; translated by Friedemann-Eckart Schwarzkopf;
    translation edited by Michael Lipson. —Rev.
        —(Anomalies)
    Translation of : Die Logosstruktur der Welt.
    Includes bibliographical references.
    ISBN 0-940262-48-7 (pbk.)
    1. Language and languages—Philosophy.   2. Consciousness.   3. Reality.
    I. Lipson, Michael.   II. Title.   III. Series.
    P106.K7913 1993   93-2286
    401—dc20   CIP

10 9 8 7 6 5 4 3 2 1

Contents

Translator's Foreword

Georg Kühlewind's *The Logos-Structure of the World* may be considered an epistemological continuation of his earlier work, *Becoming Aware of the Logos* [1]—which was written in a theological and philosophical language appropriate to the New Testament and, above all, to the Gospel of St. John.

Logos-Structure is another attempt by Kühlewind to describe his fundamental intuition—about the nature of the *word*—which runs like a connecting thread through all his works, up to and including his most recently published *Der Sprechende Mensch (The Speaking Human Being)*. [2]

For Kühlewind, the *word* is the key that allows us to decipher two riddles: the riddle of the "hieroglyph" of the human being in relationship to it's spiritual origin (which is the subject of *Becoming Aware of the Logos*), and the riddle of the human being's relationship to nature, our physical foundation, the natural environment. This is the subject of *Logos-Structure*.

The principal characteristic of the word is twofold, inner and outer. For outer sense-perception—hearing or seeing—a word appears in distinguishable sounds or letters. These sounds and letters are interpreted as *signs* if we, as perceivers, grasp that they have a *meaning*—even if we do not immediately understand that meaning. As human beings, we have the

---

1. *Becoming Aware of the Logos* (West Stockbridge, MA: Lindisfarne Press, 1985).
2. *Der Sprechende Mensch* (Frankfurt: Vittorio Klostermann, 1992).

capacity to embrace these two aspects—sounds or letters and meaning—as *one*. This capacity is the essential element that allows us to develop our humanity.

In relation to our inner spiritual source (the first riddle), we can consider the *light* of our own self-awareness as a *sign*. Yet if the light of our self-awareness is a "sign" for us, then this sign must have a "*speaker*," just as every word does. As soon as we ask about the speaker, however, we have already grasped intuitively that there might be an answer to our question.

This act of questioning is the first manifestation of the human faculty of giving and understanding *meaning*. Meaning is the inner aspect of the word, its inner side. In turning our gaze toward the one who asks and tries to answer questions we behold our own I. Whence does this I originate?

The question of the origin of the I is the fundamental gesture of conscious reflection (in German, *Besinnung.*) Who witnesses the presence of my own I's gaze? The answer is—I-AM (who is the eternal witness) witnesses the presence of my own I's gaze. I and I-AM are phenomena that can be considered in the same way that a word is—as manifestation and meaning. The Greek word *logos* signifies just this twofoldness. Indeed, considering the human ability for conscious reflection in this way leads us to the nature of the *word*, that is, to the Logos that was in the beginning, as St. John the Evangelist wrote of it.

In relation to the second riddle—the given, sense-perceptual world of nature—this same activity of conscious reflection is present in the very first question, What is *that*? Here, too, the activity of questioning is a sign for the intuition that "that" has meaning. Outer sign and inner meaning again constitute what one may call a "word." Thus the sense-perceptible world of nature is also to be considered as a text that consists of words that might have an author, the same Logos that was "in the beginning."

Epistemologically, Kühlewind justifies his approach by pointing out that every "given"—i.e., every sense-perceptible, distinguishable phenomenon—is identified as soon as consciousness says, "that." As soon as one says, "that," one *means* something. One can communicate with other human beings by agreeing what one means by "that"—a tree as timber, firewood, paper, or plant; a tree as the specific essence of a "species," or even a tree like a linguistic conjunction word, like an "and"—in which case a tree is seen as a sense-perceptible phenomenon in a life process between center and periphery, central and peripheral forces, earth and heaven.

Kühlewind shows that as far back as we can trace the evolution of language, words have continuously changed their meaning. And he shows, too, that with this change in the meaning of words, the understanding by which human communities agree on how to structure the given "that" of nature also changes in a similar way. It can be shown that in the course of the evolution of language, meaning has shrunk continuously—from an all-encompassing meaning of "tree" as a manifestation of a life force, to the modern conception of a tree as timber, fuel, or cellulose (reduced to molecular structures and DNA codes). The structure that can be found in any given evolutionary period of a language thus precisely mirrors the meaning shared by the human community living at that time. Such meaning today is called a "prevailing view" or "paradigm."

At this point, the question of the origin of language arises. What primal intuition occurred at the original arising of such a "shared vision" or paradigm of reality? This question leads to the same boundary as the focal point of the nature of the *word*.

Language is an *archetypal phenomenon* of consciousness. An "archetypal phenomenon" presents inner meaning and perceptible manifestation as *one*. If we can discover the way in which human communities structure reality, give different meanings to what they consider as "reality," then we can begin to experience the world of the Logos. "Reality" is the outer sign for the inner understanding shared by a human community. In this sense, language may be considered a model of reality.

Understanding language as a model of reality allows one to see the metamorphoses of linguistic structures as a picture of the evolution of consciousness. At the same time, this understanding of the relation between language and reality enables us to consider all aspects of nature as an integrated whole, as ancient humanity did.

From this insight, modern humanity's task arises naturally—to find a new way of integrating nature, not for our comfort or for our consumption, but as a text that has something to communicate and that has an author. If, as we attempt to decipher this text, we feel ourselves addressed by it, a new sense of creation could appear—creation as the meaning of a dialog between beginning and end.

To help us approach this task, Kühlewind ends his book with a suggestion—that we school our perception. He proposes that we can cultivate a *feeling* perception that is analogous to the *feeling* of evidence that guides all intuitive thinking and is always the last judge of the correctness and truth of a statement. In this "feeling" way of seeing, the elements of nature are integrated into a higher context in the same way that an agglomeration of single letters must be integrated to be seen as a word, and a series of words must be integrated to be read as a sentence that expresses a *single* meaning.

Kühlewind's approach may be seen as an evolution of Goethe's intuition of seeing nature as a text. Goethe wrote: "But if I would treat those cracks and fissures as letters, and try to decipher them and assemble them into words, and learn to read them, would you object?" [3]

---

3. *Wilhelm Meister.*

What was an intuitive leap for Goethe can become a systematic unfolding of our faculties. In the same way as a book
would not make sense if paper and ink were only chemically
identified, while the forms of the letters were analyzed in
terms of analytic geometry, so, too, the elements of nature are
integrated not only into systemic ecological cycles but also as
an organism whose existence utters its own sense. This corresponds to the inner understanding that makes a word into
meaning. Thus the phenomena of nature are considered both
as they *appear* and as the expression of *"meaning"*—meaning
not in the utilitarian sense of everyday consciousness but as
the spontaneous intentionality that reveals its personality
through the qualities in which it appears when it presents the
infinite possibilities of its own higher laws—which are also
manifestations of such a "speaking" intentionality.

This is why *feeling* perception is cultivated. For in feeling,
the observer's will resounds perceptibly with the conscious,
thinking grasp of the percept. And in the movement of the
attentional will in perceiving, the observer experiences the
nature of what a *substance* used to be—*"substantia"*—not
"matter" but a spiritual hierarchy, as may still be seen in the
language of Dante's *Divine Comedy*.[4] Thus the perceiver experiences in the perceptual will the force in which the complexity
of nature manifests itself.

Here the reality of *being* is felt. And thereby feeling perception becomes a mediator between our thinking conception and
the actual intentionality of the reality of nature. In the words of
Aquinas:

> *"Res naturalis, inter duos intellectus constituta."* (The
> object of nature is established between two
> intelligences.)[5]

---

4. Dante, *Paradiso* XXIX, 76 (29:76).
5. *de Veritate* qu.I, art.2.

In this same spirit Kühlewind opens his *Logos-Structure* with another quotation from Aquinas: "The reality of things is their light...." [6]

FRIEDEMANN-ECKART SCHWARZKOPF

---

6. Commentary to *Liber de causis* 1, 6.

Introduction

This book aims to show that the world, including human beings and their consciousness, is not originally a world of things but a world of words; that, fundamentally, it is structured like a text and can therefore be read like a text.

This objective makes the exposition difficult, for even the simplest descriptive statement (e.g., "the blueberries have already begun to ripen") breaks something that is simultaneous, unified, and connected into words that appear one after another and side by side. Things of consciousness—for example, problems in linguistics—are even more difficult to communicate, since many, if not all, questions appear simultaneously and need immediate answers.

This work therefore makes use of, and continuously presents to the reader, three scientific disciplines that deal with consciousness: *epistemology* (the theory of cognition), *cognitive psychology* (the psychology of cognition), and *linguistics*. The principles of the latter will probably be unfamiliar even to readers interested in spiritual science. The seeds of these disciplines may, however, be found in Rudolf Steiner's works, and I myself have discussed them more or less comprehensively, for example in *The Life of the Soul*, as well as in other works.[*]

---

[*] Georg Kühlewind, *The Life of the Soul* (Hudson, N.Y.: Lindisfarne Press, 1990) [*Das Leben der Seele*, 1982]; *Die Wahrheit Tun* ("Doing the Truth"), 1978; *Die Diener des Logos* ("Servants of the Logos"), 1981; *Das Licht des Wortes* ("Light of the Word"), 1984, all published by Verlag Freies Geistesleben in Stuttgart, Germany.

This epistemological approach attempts to take up what was given by Rudolf Steiner, but in a more differentiated way appropriate to questions being asked today. Readers may find, however, that the greatest problem may be the unaccustomed combination of these three disciplines.

This is why problems are not presented linearly. Instead, the train of thought proceeds in loops and spirals, touching repeatedly on certain themes in order to do justice to various points of view. The whole book is a *single* statement. Therefore readers will have to be patient until they have read it to the end. Much that is not discussed, or discussed insufficiently, along the way, will be explained in later sections and, ultimately, through the whole. This, at any rate, is the intention and goal.

Our method will be primarily to direct the reader's attention to phenomena of consciousness that are normally ignored and overlooked. The radical proposition that we can perceive only phenomena for which we have concepts or ideas—or for which such concepts or ideas can be developed in the course of observation—applies unconditionally to the observation of consciousness. Such observation begins with everyday consciousness. In this work we attempt to present the results of research that has made use of other planes of consciousness, in terms of the effects of these other planes of consciousness on completely observable phenomena and functions of everyday consciousness. Readers should not connect any preconceived notions or representations with the terms used here but instead form concepts and ideas anew on the basis of the text.

The methodological aim of such a study cannot be to communicate knowledge or theories; rather, it seeks to stimulate the reader's participation in the movement of thinking so that the reader can arrive at the intuitions necessary for understanding the text. Only in this way can the life of the world and of consciousness be *experienced*.

The precondition for any empiricism of consciousness is that the observer stand on a higher level of consciousness than the object of observation; otherwise unreliable conclusions and speculations will inevitably flow into the observation. Observation must proceed from the level on which we experience the world as self-evident. Only then does the observing attention, which is directed to preconscious and conscious processes of cognition, become trustworthy.

The first step in the process of observation is to distinguish between conscious cognition—guided by questioning—and the given image, which is the object of investigation and results from earlier, nonconscious cognition. A further distinction would differentiate between the planes of the present and the past in consciousness—for instance, by distinguishing between the activity of thinking and the (already past) thoughts that are the result of this activity. Observation also reveals the super-conscious nature of intuitive cognitive processes, experienced on the level of the present, as abilities or faculties. At the same time, we become aware of the impulses that stem from the soul's sphere of habit, the subconscious. This allows us to distinguish between intuitions and associations.*

It is equally important that we fully understand the difference between perception and mental representation. Because of its immediacy, perception appears to exist here and now. A mental picture or representation, on the other hand, appears more like a memory. The existential, here-and-now quality of the perceptual world can be explained only if we take into account the difference between concepts relating to natural phenomena and those relating to products of purely human

---

*See Georg Kühlewind, *Stages of Consciousness* (Hudson, N.Y.: Lindisfarne Press, 1984), chapter entitled, "The Two Stages of Consciousness," and *The Life of the Soul*, chapters 3 and 5.

activities of consciousness. Concepts produced by human beings are clear and transparent (for example, mathematical and geometrical concepts or those of man-made objects). "Concepts" that relate to nature, on the other hand, at first seem to be names, mental pictures, or collective concepts formed on the basis of external characteristics rather than the constitutive ideas of the phenomena of nature. Such constitutive ideas are unthinkable and inconceivable for normal comprehension. Mighty ideas stand behind natural phenomena— not something nonideal, as naïve thinkers believe. Just this is what gives perception its existential quality, since we ourselves are, after all, still open to these ideas. To overlook or disavow this existential quality is an aberration of theory due to inexact observation. It is the "introverted," complementary form of the same error whose "extroverted" form we see in the outer-directed focus of materialism.

The discontinuous structure of the conceptual world produces the structure of the perceptual world. Both structures are given by *language*. Language lifts the basic concepts out of what is directly given. That is one of the reasons why the *wordlike*, rather than the Idea, plays the central role in the following chapters. Because they partly appear in the sense-perceptible world and also partly live concealed as an activity of consciousness, human words can serve as a model for both human beings and the sense-perceptible world. Both receive their meaning, their hidden part, like words themselves, from human beings.

The word is the form of the idea through which there appears the word's relation to an I. The life span of the word in a human being leads from the given language (and the thinking bound to it), through abstract thinking independent of language, to meditative thinking, which is also independent of language. Meditative thinking seeks to understand words in

their primal or original meaning and remain within that understanding, or even pass beyond it. In the process, a "thinking"
develops that is adequate to the ideas of natural phenomena.
The completion, and ultimately the redemption, of the given
text of nature begins in perceptual meditation.

Meditation is the continuation of creation as it is given. If
language initially structures creation into components, then in
perceptual meditation we read creation together again—
through the accessibility of the higher word-nature. And
thereby the world receives meaning, like a text.

For the attentive observer the world will appear, in every
phase of cognitive life, to be structured by the word, or Logos.
Only an I-being has a "world." And I-beings have a world only
because the world has the nature and structure of the word, the
Logos, which in turn is accessible only to I-beings. In the first
epoch of consciousness, that of simplicity, the world is *given*
to human beings as *reality*. Percept and concept are given
together; they are separated only in a later configuration of
consciousness. Therefore in this first epoch the reality structured by the concepts provided by language is also given as a
unified whole. In the second phase of consciousness—which
ultimately leads to the emancipation of thinking from language—the given world is structured by concepts grasped by
human beings. Generally, these are abstract concepts, like
those of the natural sciences, or they may be higher, meditative
ideas. In any case, in this second reality perceiving and thinking are strictly separated; and their synthesis is no longer given
but is performed by the human being. Thus, this second reality
is also structured by the Logos; it is structured and unified
through concepts.

This applies also to the third, *potential* development of consciousness, in which human beings realize the language character of the world through their own free deeds. The language

character of the reality of the second phase or epoch is more a matter of form and not very noticeable because the functional ideas corresponding to the facts of nature are not grasped; instead, they are supplanted by the substitute concepts of measurability and calculability.

We must now learn to experience the higher ideas that are appropriate to human beings and the world by achieving higher levels of consciousness. At the same time, we must continue to develop our perceptual capacities toward *reading in the book of nature*. Then we will be able to perceive signs or letters in nature, as in a spoken or written text, instead of seeing only things. This will lead us to complete or *true reality*. The meaning of creation—the hidden part of the cosmic creative word—was to help humanity reach this point of understanding. The *new meaning*, the new reality, arises through our own continuing of creation.

One can experience that concepts and ideas always seem to *serve*—they serve as the concepts of the objects we produce for our sciences, as the cultural ideas of our education, as the artistic ideas of our self-development, or as the meditative ideas of our essential future. That the future must continuously be created—and now by us—is ancient wisdom. It was already prefigured and exemplified in the languages of the American Indians. Now this ancient wisdom begins to dawn on us again, slowly, and traveling along nearly catastrophic evolutionary paths. May the friendly warmth of the word, always based on trust, lift this ancient wisdom into modern consciousness.

Prelude

Every theory and every science begin with questions. Questions arise when we look at something twice because we were not satisfied with the first view of what we saw. That is, the existence of questions presumes two different glances, two separate views, the second of which is conscious and deliberate. These two different views necessarily originate in two different possibilities of the seeing consciousness, which can be at home on two different planes.

The first view or picture of reality is *given* to us, and it is already a picture at that moment, not a reality, as is often supposed. Reality is the last secret and can be attained only through conscious questioning. The first picture is given through the soul's superconscious and subconscious structure. It is filtered, dulled, and immobilized because of the necessary dependence of the cognizing principle in human beings on the physical organism. As a result, only a part of the totality of the world reaches conscious experience. Since our questions and answers also become a part of reality, reality is not finished or fixed: it blossoms within, and through, the human being.

Our questions concern the given picture, the first view. Epistemology deals with the question of how this "given" arises. The sciences deal with the question of how to complete, correct, and understand the given picture. And the philosophy of science deals with the question of how science is possible.

1. The Questions

....

Every question arises as a new question: it dawns on us in the same way as does insight, the answer. In fact, questions are already insights, but incomplete ones. Questions cannot develop out of naïveté; they always require duality and doubt: *What* is *that*? *That* is discovered, but at the same time we realize that it was not *fully* understood. Herein lies the paradox of asking questions: that so much must be known about what is questionable and what is to be questioned.

Questioning and cognizing presuppose the possibility of error—that is, of freedom in the process of cognition—and also presuppose the further capacity and freedom of discovering errors as such. This means that what cognizes cannot be dependent, or at least cannot be wholly dependent, upon what is to be cognized. Otherwise the result of cognizing would be predetermined by the influence of the object of cognition on the cognizing system. In that case, the lack of an independent authority would make impossible any evaluation of the results of cognition. If the cognizing system were also subject to chance events, then one and the *same* cause could lead to *different* results. And since there would be no impartial authority to evaluate these results, it would be impossible to find the "right" one among them. In this case, it would also be impossible to determine whether the cause in question was the *same*, for there would be no direct access to the causes apart from their results.

Aside from these contradictions, the phenomenon of conscious reflection—the ability of consciousness to look at itself, observe itself and describe its observations—cannot be explained through any mechanistic input-output model. If consciousness depended on influences and the reactions they trigger, it could not look at itself; self-observation would not be possible.

No mechanical system can define or describe its own mechanism while it is active. This fact refutes all theories that do not consider—or even deny—the cognitive activity that is independent of all influences, namely, the *reading* of the given. If human consciousness were indeed constituted as these theories claim it is, the theories themselves could not have come about. The connection between consciousness and the given is wordlike and ideal. The reading of a text cannot be described as the text's effect on the reader. When we read a text, only the meaning, the sense, and significance of the text, enters consciousness, not the paper or the printer's ink.

The two levels of consciousness—past and present—necessary for asking questions are inherent in *the structure of modern human consciousness*. As cognizers, we are universal; however in our noncognizing part, we are subjective. We are conscious and feel ourselves in that part of the soul where *the cognized* appears—after the process of cognition, in the "past"; but the consciousness processes—the sources of thoughts, ideas, and questions—usually remain superconscious. Intuitions—including questions, which are not *complete* intuitions—arrive superconsciously; once arrived, they become conscious.

The reflecting consciousness that is able to look at itself has two planes, the past and the present. The past continually derives from the present. The soul oscillates between these two planes, barely touching the upper one, the present. It is this oscillation that enables the soul to ask questions and to look both at itself and at the plane of the past. This is the basic duality through which the paradox of questioning is realized. The answer lies in pursuing the intuition of the question.

2. The Given

....

One of the basic gestures of the *consciousness soul* is to observe its own contents. Its potential is realized and becomes effective only by means of this gesture: "In sensations and thoughts, the soul loses itself to other things; as consciousness soul, however, it takes hold of its own being."[1]

Therefore the consciousness soul may also be called "*self-*consciousness soul."[2]

In the process of taking hold of its own being, the consciousness soul *comes into being.* And this process of taking hold begins with observations in, and of, consciousness itself.

Reflection on Consciousness

When we begin to reflect on consciousness, we discover its processes, as well as their results—we find thinking, perceiving, speaking, as well as concepts, percepts, words. We can notice that these processes and contents already existed, or arose, prior to reflection. Even the *ability* to reflect is *given*, though the *act* of reflection itself is a free deed. Were this deed also given and not free, the given as such could not be discovered.

---

1. Rudolf Steiner, *An Outline of Occult Science* (GA 13) (Hudson, N.Y.: Anthroposophic Press, 1989), chapter "The Nature of Humanity."
2. Rudolf Steiner, *Metamorphoses of the Soul*, vol. 1 (GA 59) (London: Rudolf Steiner Press, 1983), lecture of October 28, 1909.

The discovery that the human faculties are *given* and that we did not produce them by ourselves can call forth wonder, gratitude, and joy in us—joy in the existence of consciousness, in the ability to turn attention to any theme we choose, joy in this autonomy. This joy, which is kindled by the above experience and not by the mental picture of it, is the soul's best starting point for a schooling of consciousness.

Epistemological Consideration of the Given

The given precedes every question; it is the first image from which questions emerge or are kindled. The *given* is everything that appears in consciousness without any activity of thought or memory.[3]

This means that the given image of the outer and inner world changes in the course of our life according to our circumstances; therefore, too, it can vary from individual to individual.[4]

What is given, or (pure) experience, includes both what we *later* call the "perceptual image"—*after* we have defined it as such by thinking—and the inner world that has not yet been processed by thinking. Thus we can call the given "the appearance to the senses," if by "senses" we mean not only those directed outward but also those that grasp the events of our inner life of soul and consciousness.[5]

---

3. Rudolf Steiner, *A Theory of Knowledge* (GA 2, p. 27ff) (Hudson, N.Y.: Anthroposophic Press, 1978), pp. 14,15.
4. See Steiner, *Truth and Knowledge* (GA 3, p.47ff) (Blauvelt, N.Y.: Rudolf Steiner Publications, 1981), pp. 53,54.
5. See Steiner, *A Theory of Knowledge* (GA 2, p. 241), p. 16; and *Anthroposophie: Ein Fragment* ("Anthroposophy: A Fragment") (GA 45) (Dornach, Switzerland: Rudolf Steiner Verlag, 1980), chapter 2.

For an adult, the given perceptual picture is an accumulation of details, juxtaposed in space and successive in time, an agglomeration of disconnected objects of sensation.[6]

That particulars (things, for instance) appear as given is a consequence of *preceding*—not present—conceptual determinations, as a result of super-conscious, previous "instruction of the senses" (whereby concepts become integrated in the senses—see below p. 40 ff). In other words, adults do not have to reflect anew each time they see an object they have seen before: they already see it conceptually.

The same is true for sensory qualities. The high conceptuality corresponding to sensory qualities, which surpasses the concepts of objects in scope and vitality, is "formed" in childhood through superconscious intuitions. When a child begins to distinguish colors, no change occurs in the physical organization of its eyes; rather, the child grasps the idea of color itself, or of individual colors.

We can also reflect on the contents of consciousness as such, regardless of their potential reference to the perceptual world. We find memory pictures (representations), fantasy images, words, sentences, thoughts, emotions, wishes, and so on. If current thinking ceases, this world, too, is a conglomeration of unconnected details.

The distinction between what is given and what we actually cognize may be made in different ways. When one articulates a theory of knowledge (an epistemology), one must examine the origin and development of the adult's given image of the world and *conceive the idea of the given quite radically*. This means artificially removing—in a thought experiment—the

---

6. See Steiner, *A Theory of Knowledge* (GA2, pp. 30-32), pp. 17-19; and *The Philosophy of Freedom* (GA 4, pp. 60, 89, 94, 137) (Hudson, N.Y.: Anthroposophic Press, 1986), pp. 50, 78, 83, 84, 125.

concepts already contained in the given. Once we have removed all concepts, the connections between objects, "things," separate details, and even the objects of sensation, disappear. Only an undifferentiated continuum devoid of any structure remains,[7] for the separation of any particular individual detail out of the whole undifferentiated given image is already an act of thinking activity.[8]

By means of this thought experiment, the boundary between the given and what is consciously cognized is drawn most deeply. The unstructured continuum given in this way is called the "directly given." This "directly given" is not part of normal experience but an artificial extrapolation that serves to help us better understand experience.

Examination of the Given from the Standpoint of Cognitive Psychology

How does the given appear in consciousness? "The first form in which the whole comes to meet us stands finished before us. We have no part in its coming into being. As if springing forth from an unknown Beyond, reality first offers itself to the grasp of our senses and our minds."[9]

This "unknown Beyond" may be identified as the superconscious, spiritual part of the human soul.[10]

From this part of the soul, the specifically human faculties—thinking, perceiving, and speaking—are given to us. The course or processes of these faculties are superconscious; but the results are *conscious*. The given consists of these results. The

---

7. See Steiner, *Truth and Knowledge* (GA 3, p. 45ff), pp. 52,53.
8. Ibid, (GA 3, p. 46, fn. p.60), p. 52.
9. See Steiner, *A Theory of Knowledge* (GA 2), chapter entitled "Experience."
10. See Kühlewind, *The Life of the Soul*, chapters 2 and 5; See Steiner, *A Theory of Knowledge*, p.14

processes by which the given is given is superconscious. In earlier epochs of the evolution of consciousness human beings actually experienced this giving, and today children still experience it when learning to speak.

Since the "first form" of reality enters consciousness already *finished* as we become aware of it, we can almost experience— we may call it a "boundary experience"—that the processes that "give" this reality occur superconsciously. After all, for there to be "finished" results, processes must have occurred first. We do not know how we speak, nor how sounds are formed, nor how the grammar and syntax of our mother tongue—never fully described or describable—are acquired in early childhood; nor do we know how a perception comes about.

Even thinking is to be found within the given,[11] even though it is the activity in which we participate most consciously because we ourselves produce it. Thinking does not appear without our active participation. Yet it is in no way *arbitrary* or *subjective*: it has its own inherent lawfulness, its own nature, which is manifest in its *how*, its logic. Thus thinking is not only formally given, but how it proceeds, its lawfulness, is *produced superconsciously*. Its rules are not consciously formulated and they can never be exhaustively described. In this sense, thinking is *superconsciously given.*[12]

Because the "how" of thinking originates in the superconscious and is therefore given to us, we cannot debate its correctness—except on the basis of this same thinking that is now in doubt.[13]

We can observe thinking and contemplate its nature only after it is there: given.

---

11. See Steiner, *Truth and Knowledge* (GA 3, pp.53-55), pp.58-61.
12. See Steiner, *Theory of Knowledge* (GA 2, pp. 29,48,49,52), pp. 16, 35, 36, 39.
13. See Steiner, *Truth and Knowledge* (GA 3, p. 59), p. 64; and *The Philosophy of Freedom* (GA 4, pp. 34, 49, 53f, 60, 62, 86, 90), pp.22, 37, 40-41, 50, 51-52, 75-80.

All these activities, including mental picturing (representation), are actually *faculties* for doing something without knowing how to do it. This *ability* enables us to initiate processes in consciousness, although we are not conscious of the processes but only of their results. This is similar to our voluntary body movements: we set the body in motion with our will and chart the course of its movement in a mental image. Then we perceive the result, but we do not consciously follow the act of the movement in its "how."

Such human faculties are given from "above," from the spiritual plane, and they intervene in the living and sentient body to express and articulate themselves in it. The way these faculties are given to us changes in the course of the development of the individual and of humanity as a whole (see chapter 8). It is characteristic of contemporary adults that the connection between consciousness and its superconscious sources is interrupted by an abyss or gap that divides the plane of the past from that of the present.[14]

Observation of the Given Functions of Consciousness

Each of the three basic functions of consciousness—perceiving, thinking, and speaking (which are the basis also of other human faculties)—has a distinct character and is experienced differently by adults today. Perception, for instance, poses many riddles. The disjointed particulars of perception immediately provoke questions; they are not at all transparent or comprehensible to contemporary perceiving.

The difference in the "givenness" of perceiving and thinking lies not only in that perceiving is mediated through the

---

14. See Kühlewind, *Das Licht des Wortes*, chapter 1.

senses while new concepts, new thoughts, appear in consciousness through intuition; much more significant is the fact
that thoughts and concepts are only wholly comprehensible
and transparent to us when they are really thought. Though we
can certainly say things we do not understand, we cannot possibly think anything we do not understand thoroughly. Nothing
remains hidden in the finished thought; so there is nothing
more to search for in it once it has been thought.[15]

Therefore, we are justified in taking a "naïve" point of view
in regard to thinking. The logic and self-evident nature of
thinking—its *how*—are given from the superconscious sphere,
and, in this "givenness," it is totally transparent and comprehensible. Indeed, anything we understand, we understand only
when it is "explained" through thinking, through ideas. In the
case of thinking, empiricism is sufficient. Attempts to become
aware of the "how" of thinking through logic—which can
never be sufficient—do not replace the necessity of entering
into the living stream of thinking if we are to understand anything, even logic.

The perceptual world is also structured by concepts, and
only because of that can we experience or perceive it. Only
concepts can mark the boundaries of particulars, can say that
they are things, that there are particulars, defining them as
such. Human experience is always structured; reflection or
contemplation always starts with an already-structured image
of the world. How does this primary structure, given through
concepts—which are themselves given—come about prior to
any self-conscious cognitive activity?

This question turns our observing attention to the third
basic "given," namely, *language*. Language teaches us to
understand discontinuously given signs and symbols, that is,

---

15. See Steiner, *Philosophy of Freedom*, p. 91-92.

to think in concepts and to perceive discrete particulars, and hence structuring in general.

Though language appears to us as a perceptual phenomenon, it can be as transparent and understandable as thinking. Language consists of perceptible acoustic or optic *signs for our understanding.* Understanding (meaning) is the hidden part of language. It does not appear in the perceptual world but occurs—through intuition—in the human spirit. The reality or totality of language includes both the signs and their understanding; neither is *by itself* the reality of language. *Language unites in itself the cognitive elements of perceptual reality that would otherwise appear separately.* When we do not understand them, the "signs" are not signs but remain mere objects of perception that we can puzzle over. They are signs only when they mean something besides themselves. When we understand them, the meaning we comprehend absorbs the signs; as objects of perception, they become unimportant and uninteresting. Voices, words; the form, size, structure, and material of the letters—all these disappear as objects of perception: they are dissolved and *read.*

In children, language induces primary perceiving and primary thinking as a unity in a monistic and undivided way, and they remain united until thinking emancipates itself from language. Children learn their first language, their mother tongue, "monistically." They do not just impose "names" on objects and meanings, as nominalistic and naïve thinkers imagine. Rather, language—and the concepts it provides— structure inner and outer worlds into objects, phenomena, and meanings. Human language, which is always discontinuous and consists of sounds, words, and sentences, *structures* our faculty of understanding, thus making it earthly-human—that is, discontinuous and conceptual. *That is why the world is "given" to us already structured into discrete particulars* like a text, and human beings only *become* fully human by gradually learning to "read together" these particulars.

The awakening of our first language occurs very differently from the learning of a second language. Learning a second language is a dualistic process because we have already been given the meaning in our (first) mother tongue, and we then merely learn the more or less corresponding expression in the second language. The first language *creates* the meanings that are then "named" in the second language. In fact, this process reinforces the impression that the world is built up nominalistically because we easily forget that we can perceive a thing only if it already has a meaning, only if it is already defined by a concept. *Before* the first language or mother tongue, there is nothing that could be named.

In the "energetic" phase (Wilhelm von Humboldt) of the evolution of language, in which language structures the world, *thinking and language are still one.* As long as this is the case, the perceptual world cannot become independent of language, and object, word, and concept are undivided. This is reflected in numerous traditions that describe the creation of the world through the divine Word: the idea is uttered, and creation enters into existence. In this state of consciousness the perceptual world is like a continuation, or a part, of language. Therefore, at this stage language is not yet puzzling: *there are not yet any other concepts besides the ones language gives,* and they structure the world. In this state of *innocence,* questions cannot yet be asked.

In general, questions—and with questions, science—are possible only after thinking has emancipated itself from its teacher, namely, language. This emancipation takes place in the epoch of the consciousness soul. In earlier times, the pursuit of science was the privilege of a few chosen individuals, precursors of our age, who partially exemplified and foreshadowed the structure of the consciousness soul.[16]

With the exception of this elite, who anticipated later developmental stages, everything was still given to people at this earlier stage in the evolution of consciousness. Today the world is given to us in a different way. In the more dreamlike phase of consciousness, people experienced as given even the cognitive processes that have now moved into the realm of the superconscious. The given we are conscious of today is on the plane of finished thoughts, finished perceptions; that is, on the plane of the past. In earlier times, this plane was considered to be merely the final point of the experienced, given world. Nowadays, however, impulses from the subconscious, all of which are destructive for our soul life, have joined these finished thoughts and perceptions. This is the field that psychology deals with (see chapter 8).

Regarding Concepts

The term "thinking" covers several very different activities of consciousness. The highest achievement of thinking is the intuitive grasping or understanding of a *new idea,* a new concept—"new" in the sense that the thinker is thinking it for the first time. Every true understanding is new.

Contemplation immediately reveals that we cannot easily say what a concept is. To do so we would have to use concepts—the very thing we want to characterize—which would

---

16. Rudolf Steiner, "The Human Soul and the Evolution of the World," lecture 5 (ms. translation), (GA 212, lecture of May 7, 1922).

assume that *in practice* we already "know" what a concept is. Thus we become aware that most concepts are already given to us when we begin to direct attention to them and are not formed through our own conscious reflection. Concepts represent an *ability*, rather than a knowledge. This ability reveals itself in our being able to recognize every table, chair, pencil, and so on, as such once we have understood the *functional concept* that corresponds to it. For example, when we use the lid of a piano as a surface to write or eat on, we realize that the lid is now being used as a "table." A pen can be used as a weapon for stabbing, and then it is a stiletto. To produce the *pure concept* of a man-made object, however, is not so easy. To do so we would have to reproduce the understanding that enables us to identify all tables as such, as well as all objects that can function as tables. To do this is to understand the function of a table; or it is the result of this understanding. This ability is superconscious, as are all other specifically human abilities, such as thinking, speaking, perceiving, and intentional movements. We don't know *how* we do it.

In the schooling of consciousness, the goal of the exercise of concentration or the control of thoughts is precisely to lead us to this intuitive understanding, to the reproduction of the *pure concept*[17]—the conscious reproduction of what we learned unconsciously in childhood. Thus, from this first observation we realize that concepts are intuitive—that, in contrast to mental images or representations, they cannot be remembered.

The second discovery reveals the distinction between concept and word. For adults the line separating them is sharp and

17. See Kühlewind, *Stages of Consciousness*, chapter entitled "Concentration and Contemplation."

clear. A word designates something we understand or have understood in a language. We can easily understand the function of an object, for example, a pair of scissors, without naming the object. This distinction between word and concept is *today* easy to comprehend; however, prior to the possibility of the consciousness soul, it could not have been grasped because thinking was then not yet emancipated from language.

This is still true for very young children—for them language and thinking are intertwined. Distinguishing between concept and word requires that we are able to look at consciousness. Immature reflection may draw the distinction between concept and word falsely—not between concept and word but between *thing* and word—not realizing that only its concept makes a thing *this* thing. Then nominalism arises. A thing is pictured without its concept, and the word is regarded as identical with the concept. Therefore, nominalism assumes that the concept is only a *name,* a way of naming an object. It is not noticed that we can only name something we have first grasped conceptually. Nominalism introduced into the realm of human thought the idea that things could exist without concepts. This is a truly inconceivable, unthinkable idea, yet it has decisively influenced not only the natural sciences (and through them the other sciences) but also the whole of Western Christian thinking. This thinking has become so used to "thinking" the unthinkable that the criteria of thinkability and self-evidence have been lost. What has been lost above all is the *experience* of understanding, of thinking-intuition as the essence of the concept.

A second source of nominalism can also be discovered today quite easily. Compare the functions of man-made objects with things and phenomena in nature. We can understand the functions of man-made objects, and even mathematical and geometrical concepts are transparent to us, but our relationship to things and phenomena in nature is very different. We do not know their *constitutive* or functional ideas. The "functions" of feldspar, lilies, or turtles are unknown to us, and we have learned not to ask about them any more. We classify and identify the things of nature according to their outer characteristics. For example, plants with a certain number of sepals and stamens in their blossoms belong to the family of the *Rosaceae, roses*. We do not understand *functionally* what this means, and we cannot be sure that the same characteristics always belong to the same function. The way we proceed concerning natural objects is similar to classifying pieces of furniture according to the number of legs or doors, regardless of their purpose. In other words, we relate to nature in a truly nominalistic way. For us the concepts of natural objects are simply collective terms derived from external attributes, or—to put it more precisely—they are universalized representational mental images. Of course, "wolf," "rose," "quartz crystal," and so on are true universals: we have no reason to assume that they come into being without concepts, when we know for sure that not even a button could be made without a concept. However, nowadays people are unable to grasp the vast, living, sentient ideas of natural phenomena, at least not without a schooling of their consciousness.

Thus, in the universals—the ideas of nature—we are faced with something we cannot grasp; *initially* our powers of consciousness do not suffice to grasp them. The ideas of natural objects are too bright, too blinding, to be grasped by dialectical consciousness. Understanding them requires that we can "read in the book of nature."

Functional understanding must be distinguished from identifying a thing on the basis of external characteristics or mental pictures. If we disregard this distinction, we fail to notice that we have no adequate concepts for nature, but only mental pictures that help us orient ourselves according to the *outside surface* of phenomena. The statement "This is a columbine" means that the appearance of the plant fits with what we know to be characteristic of columbines. Nevertheless, we see or perceive phenomena only because we have concepts; we comprehend the outer characteristics and qualities of the plant—such as the color, form, size, number of stamens—conceptually. These concepts stand in, so to speak, for the natural phenomenon's concepts and thus allow us to categorize and identify it. Still, they are merely substitute concepts and not the functional or creative ideas that correspond to, and are, the essence of the phenomenon.

Since the external characteristics of natural phenomena are so clearly "super-ficial" ["above the surface"], our understanding of concepts has become falsified. We have forgotten that concepts above all, and in their essence, consist of *understanding*. Therefore we seek the essential of the concept in the direction of *abstraction*. The "essential" and "common" properties and characteristics of the objects of perception are derived from the individual object through abstraction. However, abstraction presupposes knowledge of the concept. To determine the "essential and common" characteristics and thereby to define or limit the individual objects under consideration—in other words, to "select" them out—requires a norm. This norm is the concept.[18]

This abstraction model of concepts emphasizes their generality, in contrast to the particular individual object of perception. Whereas the universals of scholasticism—which are ideas based on understanding—could express themselves in particulars as *universalia in re*, the abstract concept, on the other hand, can hardly, if at all, be seen in the individual object; nor can it help us to grasp individual details. For exam-

---

18. See Steiner, *A Theory of Knowledge* (GA 2), chapter 10 entitled "The Inner Nature of Thinking."

ple, "green" as an abstract concept cannot cover a particular perception of green; but "green," as the intuitively understood universal, contains all shades of the color. To teach children what "green" is, we by no means have to show them all the shades of a color. Once a child has grasped the idea of "green" by means of a single green, that child will correctly identify all shades of this color as "green" without having to think about it—an experience we will return to later on.

The more we consider concepts as abstractions, the more they will seem to lack in being, compared to the concrete particular we perceive. This tendency is reinforced by the existential, "being" character of perception, which contrasts sharply with the unreality of finished thoughts and concepts. Thoughts seem to be so independent of reality that we can think or imagine anything at all, whenever and wherever we want. Perception, on the other hand, can occur only in the present moment, a truth that is a great puzzle for epistemology. We will discuss it in chapter 5.

Consideration of how we proceed when we want to understand something reveals the difference between concepts of man-made objects and concepts of nature. For example, when we want to understand the concepts "shoe sole" or "ball-point pen," we try to comprehend the function of these objects. We do not start by analyzing them; we are interested in the component parts and materials only when we want to produce them. When we are dealing with natural objects, however, we proceed in the other direction and analyze them first, if possible down to their smallest particles. In most cases, we do not even ask about the function of these natural objects. In any case, analysis cannot tell us anything about function. In fact, we have so completely forgotten to consider the purpose or meaning of objects in nature that we equate a mathematical description of them with truly understanding them. This is like trying to understand a page of text by mathematically determining the position of the black and white points on its surface rather than by reading it.

The difference between the comprehension of the concepts of man-made objects and that of the concepts of natural objects is rarely noticed. We interpret the incomprehensible aspect of natural objects as a lack of concepts and confound higher ideas with what is idea-less. This leads to catastrophic results in our spiritual life, which can be summarized as follows:

1. The true nature of the idea, of the concept, was misunderstood; and the fact that it is based on *understanding* was forgotten.

2. The unthinkable notion—the nonthought—of "property-less" matter (Giordano Bruno), able to act as bearer of various properties, was introduced: matter without form, being without idea. This notion now haunts philosophy and the sciences in many variations—as the thing-in-itself, as the subconscious or unconscious, as the foundation of the world and of consciousness, as elementary particles without qualities, and so on. Because of all this, we imagine the perceptual world and its elements as conceptless.

3. The notion that concepts arise by abstraction leads to the opposition of their generality to the concrete—supposedly idea-less—qualities of separate things.

4. Understanding, the foundation of all theories and in its essence absolute and irreducible, has been pushed into the background—or we have postulated various mechanisms to explain it. Mechanical causality became the only explanatory principle.

5. Instead of interpreting phenomena as letters to be read, analysis was defined as the only justified cognitive method.

6. The contradictions inherent in the five developments listed here obstruct the healthy circulation of the life of our consciousness just as impenetrable occlusions prevent the free flow of blood in the body. As a result, our thinking and cognitive faculties are no longer healthy. The most obvious symptoms of this affliction are theories and thoughts that cancel each other out, and our failure to notice this. Examples of such thoughts are: "thinking is subjective," "thinking is a mechanism or a natural process," or "human consciousness is determined."

The Given and the Activity of the Senses: Instruction of the Senses

Because *reflecting* consciousness is a *thinking* consciousness, everything in it is permeated with concepts. In this state of conscious reflection we are most awake. However, we are not always reflecting, and therefore we can find, in retrospect, events that do not seem to be permeated with concepts, for example, soul moods, emotions, unrest, and so on. Thus, beside or below wakeful thinking consciousness, whose contents the I can remember, one can perceive a second, sentient, yet only semiconscious and more dreamlike layer of consciousness. The contents of this second layer elude the grasp of the self-conscious I. Nevertheless, insofar as a certain content of consciousness is a distinct THAT—whether arrived at through perception [including inner perception], mental representation, or thinking—it is always interwoven with concepts. Without concepts there would be no THAT because we could not distinguish it from its surroundings. Concepts separate THAT out of its surroundings, making it available for outer or inner perception.

Even though only what is conceptual can enter thinking consciousness, this same consciousness—in flagrant self-contradiction—speaks of the existence of nonconceptual, idea-less things. Nonconceptual things were first "discovered" in the realm of sensory perception; later they were transferred to a "transcendental" cosmic realm, beyond the reach of thinking consciousness. What resulted were inherently self-contradictory constructs of *thought*—no one ever actually *saw* a "thing-in-itself" or the "subconscious"—which would also have to be tested by thought. This contradiction, testing nonideal constructs through thinking, already contains its own verdict.

Let us now look more closely at the field of sense perception.

We can perceive because of our given senses. These consist of a sense organ—which can be more or less localized in the organism—and an *organization of consciousness*, which is teachable and without which the sense organ does not function. Consciousness contributes the conceptual part to sense perception—both in a child's perception of color, for instance, and in the givenness of particulars or individual objects of sensation. Without this contribution—as we saw when we artificially removed all concepts in a thought experiment—there remains only an unstructured continuum.

As adults, we receive from the senses—as raw material for thinking—a picture consisting of particulars. This picture is already structured conceptually before any *current* thinking activity begins. In fact, we can observe that when adults perceive something with which they are *sufficiently familiar*, they "simply and immediately" recognize it for what it is—for example, as table or pencil—without thought or memory. However, if, for example, we do not know the functional concept "table," and do not develop it on the basis of perception, we do not see a table but only a smooth wooden surface with legs and so on—provided we at least know these latter concepts.

Descartes already observed that adults perceive conceptually. However, as in the case above, substitute concepts hide this fact when they take the place of missing concepts—for instance, when people describe a fork as "a piece of metal with five pointed ends." Obviously, we have to distinguish between *perception*—as an activity that can lead to an experience of the I[19]—and the merely emotional *reaction* (astral experience) to a sensory quality or an object (see chapter 5).

Rudolf Steiner describes the senses as physical *and* spiritual organs through which "an insight is gained without the participation of the intellect, memory, etc." Obviously the "etc." here refers to any current, intentional activity of consciousness. Therefore insight or knowledge gained through the senses is "simple and immediate" and *"precedes* any evaluation or judgment; it is a sensation just as colors and warmth are sensations."[20]

Insights (cognitions), however, are always interwoven with concepts, as we have seen in the simple examples given above. Consequently, the senses themselves must be conceptually schooled so as to be able to produce insight since all other current activities of consciousness, including memory, are excluded from pure sense activity.

It is very difficult for people today who, consciously or unconsciously, think materialistically to understand that even sensory qualities cannot be perceived without concepts. Nevertheless, observation provides us with sufficient proof for this. We have already discussed how children learn to distinguish colors. When we teach handicapped children about the

---

19. See Steiner, *Anthroposophie: Ein Fragment*, (GA 45, chapter 6).
20. Ibid., (GA 45, pp. 35ff, chapter 2 and *Theory of Knowledge*, (GA 2, chapter 7).

smoothness or roughness of a surface by letting them touch it, we are not "teaching" their fingers but instructing them in the *formation of concepts*. As speech therapists know, children who cannot reproduce a speech sound, or who can do so only incorrectly (lisping), must first be taught to hear this sound accurately and correctly. They hear the sound properly not because of some change in their sense organ (their ears) but because they grasp the sound's configuration. That is, they *conceptually* separate the sound from its form, its pitch, and its other qualities, thereby grasping the specific character of the sound that differentiates it from all others.

This conceptual component of perception is even more pronounced in the experience of identifying colors, as in the example mentioned above. Once we have grasped the concept "green," we can identify *all* variant shades of this color as green without recourse to mental pictures or memory, which are already given and could therefore not help us recognize new shades of green we have not seen before. Clearly, even if children first encounter the functional concept "table" in a small, round, brown, one-legged wooden table of normal height, they will nevertheless later be able to identify, as a table, a large, rectangular, white metal table with x-shaped legs and modern, low design. If they tried comparing the second table with the remembered image of the first one, they would actually be misled.

Our ability to differentiate within a qualitative field (for instance, in the field of color through the sense of sight) means that this qualitative field can be structured conceptually and that the sense in question has intuitively integrated these concepts. The same applies to differentiation between qualitative fields. Without conceptual learning such differentiation is impossible, and we remain at the level of mere sensitive reaction.

As we can experience in the perception of speech sounds, the three higher senses—the sound- or word-sense; the concept- or thought-sense; and the you- or I-sense (the sense for another I-being)—apprehend only pure ideas. The other senses (for example, that of hearing) provide the "raw material" for the higher senses. This raw material is then (in the case of the sense of hearing) processed by the sense of sound (or word-sense, i.e., sense for the acoustical *form* of a movement, which in turn passes the product of its activity on to the sense of thought, and so on.[21]

Clearly, the higher senses have to be taught to perceive the specifically human properties for which they *are* the senses. Their work is purely ideational. They are "addressed" when we learn to speak, and their spiritual sense organism is developed by means of this instruction. As a result, they are able to perceive sounds, concepts, and I-ness "simply and directly," like a sensation. The instruction proceeds from the activity of the I. *New* sounds, *new* thoughts, *new* I-beings are always recognized as such by current intuitions or the activity of consciousness. *Initially*, the new perceptions are not at all "simple and direct" for these senses, as we can clearly see in the experience of children as well as of adults when, for example, they learn a foreign language. The sounds, concepts, and I-perceptions that are already rooted in our consciousness, and our experience and proficiency in apprehending ideas in these areas, help us to absorb the new.

Our I-being also instructs our other senses and equips them with conceptuality, so that, in sensory activity, the senses can perceive "conceptually." As adults this is also true for the

---

21. See Kühlewind, "Das Wahrnehmen räumlicher und zeitlicher Formen" ("The Perception of Spatial and Temporal Forms") in *Das Goetheanum* no. 21, (May 24, 1984). Available as chapter 14, *Schooling of Consciousness* (Fair Oaks, California: Rudolf Steiner College Publications, 1985).

particulars we perceive without having a word or name for them. For example, we see totally irregular solids or two-dimensional forms in qualitatively the same way as we perceive spheres or circles. This is significantly not the case in children; they see and draw in a simplified manner in accordance with the concepts they have already acquired.

Our difficulty in realizing that the (pre-consciously) instructed senses perceive conceptually is above all due to the fact, already discussed, that we relate differently to man-made objects than we do to natural phenomena. Sensory qualities, too, also belong to the class of natural phenomena; their "concepts" are merely a pale reflection of their meaning or message, which cannot be conceived by everyday consciousness. Something of their high *ideality* appears in the arts. But we must never forget that everything that is nameable is defined and determined by an idea. Of course, we are not used to imagining other than man-made concepts in this way. Nevertheless, any natural object also exemplifies this fact of determination by idea. For instance, we do not "understand" the idea of the lily—the plant's appearance is not fixed once and for all but changes with the seasons, the weather, and the soil quality—but the *species* is fixed. This idea of the species differs qualitatively from that of the "cup," partly because the former is alive. When we recognize a plant as a lily it is not because of the functional idea, which we do not know, but because of substitute concepts, (shape, color, smell); or, when we are faced by an unusual variety of lily, we may perhaps carefully compare our perception with our mental image; we usually perform such a comparison when we collect mushrooms in the woods, for example. Between these two extreme cases—recognition on the basis of functional concepts or recognition on the basis of substitute concepts and memory images—lies a continuous spectrum of sensory processes in which mental representation supplements sensory activity.

The middle senses function in a specifically human way, for we do not simply react to sounds, colors, smells, and so on, but rather we understand our perceptions as I-experiences that can then become the basis for judgment in the I.[*] This specifically *human* functioning of the middle senses is due to their instruction, their equipment with concepts, which makes them receptive for everything *wordlike*.

Our senses would not function, however, without our specifically human *attention*—an attention that can attend to a wordlike, conceptually structured perceptual world because the fundamental concepts that structure sensory qualities, as well as other concepts, have been instilled in us. In fact, these concepts structuring the qualitative field of a particular sense belong to the *sense organism*. After the senses have been instructed, they receive perceptions as *given*. This is nowhere so striking as in the experience or practice of the arts. Here, our attention is like the breath flowing through a wind instrument; it takes on the configuration of air according to the guidance by the player. In the same way, depending upon how they have been instructed, the configuration of attention is formed differently in each of the senses.

Without instruction, without being instilled with concepts, the senses are "senses for" qualities; they embody the possibility of reacting to colors, sounds, and so on, and the possibility of being instructed. The education of the senses *actualizes* our potential to perceive colors, sounds, tastes, and so on in a human way. A small child is still *wholly* sense

---

*See footnote 19.

organ[22]—the perceptual field is not yet divided into twelve discontinuous bands or strips, with no transition between them. This division of the perceptual field arises through the human speaking environment, although, except in the case of the higher senses, this division is partly predetermined by the organism. The fabric of the sensory world is "woven," as it were: first the warp of the high concepts of the sensory qualities is introduced; then the woof of the other concepts of objects and phenomena is added to it.

We grasp only the conceptual part of our perceptual world. Whether nature itself is an ideal construct, whether the fabric of the sensory world is indeed structured like a text—or merely consists of *things* rather than of signs—will become clear when we discuss the idea of reality in greater detail.

---

22. Rudolf Steiner, lecture of May 26, 1922 (GA 212), available as *The Human Heart* (Spring Valley, N.Y.: Mercury Press, 1985); (GA 218, lecture of November 19, 1922); and *A Modern Art of Education* (GA 307) (Hudson, N.Y.: Anthroposophic Press, 1972), lecture of August 10, 1923.

3. The First Structuring of the Given

....

The given inner and outer picture of the world presents itself to self-reflection as already structured—that is, permeated with concepts: we see it as made up of particulars. Even the cognitive functions of consciousness already exist when we turn our observing attention toward them. We have called the source of these functions the *super*conscious, in order to distinguish the source of cognition from the *sub*conscious, which consists of *noncognitive* elements in the soul.[23]

The two realms of the superconscious and the subconscious—both of which are *unconscious*—are often confused in psychological discussion, or looked upon as the same power source, which is a sign of our inability to distinguish spirit and soul. The superconscious is the spiritual part of the soul.

Reflection finds not only the world content structured but also finds the human being in its existence structured in such a way that the world is given in dualities. For example, reflection finds a world consisting of particulars, and we find ourselves facing and opposing it as perceivers. Similarly, in our being we find inner experiences, thoughts, and concepts, and insofar as we "find" them, we sense the presence of a subject facing this "preexisting" inner world—at least occasionally. As soon as we have experiences, these are structured and contain boundaries, details, unities.

---

23. See Kühlewind, *The Life of the Soul*, chapter 3.

If we were to strip our given picture of the world of all concepts, this would leave only an unstructured continuum,[24] which could no longer be called *experience*.[25]

At the same time, however, the separation of subject and object would disappear. The term "subject" here refers merely to the *place* of the experience; both thinking and perceiving provide the subject with something universal and intersubjective. To deny this with regard to thinking would be naïve and self-contradictory. Even perception is only subjective in that different individuals' different and unique points of view in relation to the object—their different sensory capacities, sets of concepts, and differing abilities to conceptualize—influence the given picture. Nevertheless, there can be no doubt that we live in a shared perceptual world. Indeed, we cannot even *discuss* this doubt because such a discussion and its subject matter presuppose a shared perceptual world. By the same token, however, we cannot tell with absolute certainty whether the sensory qualities we perceive—for example, the colors we see—are exactly the same as everyone else perceives.

Formulating the Question

Our sensory and spiritual organization determines the structure of the given we perceive.[26]

This same organization also causes us to experience the given as split into perception separated into subject and

24. See Steiner, *Truth and Knowledge* (GA 3, pp.45-46), pp. 51, 52.
25. Ibid., p. 52. Also (GA 3, fn. p. 60).
26. See Steiner, *Philosophy of Freedom* (GA 4, pp. 64-65, 89, 96, 113, 126, 130, 132), pp. 53-54, 78, 85, 101, 114-115, 118, 119-120.

object[27] in such a way that we consider our inner life—of thinking, feeling, and willing—as part of the subject and the perceptual world as part of the object.[28] The distinction is, of course, not exact, but it will do for the purpose of our discussion here.

Our inner world is likewise similarly structured in its givenness. Naturally, then, we have to wonder how this preexisting *structure*, without which we would not experience anything consciously, arose. We have to ask, too, what our own human "organization" signifies and what its purpose is.

The Structure of the Found or Given

If we look more closely at inner and outer reality as it is given, we find that each consists of discrete particulars, facts, things, and processes, as well as of connections and relationships between the particulars. Without exception, these particulars are distinguished and contrasted from each other and their environment or background by means of *concepts*. The relations between the particulars are all such that they do *not* belong to the perceptual realm. For example, qualities characterized by adjectives—such as small, big, similar, crooked, here, there, and so on—are *purely conceptual determinations* arising from the perceived particulars by comparison or other operations of thought.

Nevertheless, for the most part such characteristic qualities as size and so on are integrated into our senses. Therefore we easily fall into thinking them to be original, *a priori* parts of

27. See Steiner, *Philosophy of Freedom* (GA 4, pp. 88, 112, 247), pp. 77, 100, 235; (GA 78, lecture of August 29, 1921), summarized in *Fruits of Anthroposophy* (London: Rudolf Steiner Press, 1986), pp.7-8.
28. Ibid., (GA 4, pp. 125, 126, 132), pp. 114, 115, 119.

our sensory activity and therefore of a nonconceptual character. But this view would have to assume a *present* mental picturing, judgment, or memory of each time we perceive a
thing—which clearly contradicts our observation that when we
see familiar objects, they are already conceptually defined.

Ultimately, all particulars, even those that are designated
by nouns in the European languages, dissolve into relationships. We can trace the return of our consciousness to the
"directly given" through an example. When we say, "This tree
is bigger than that one," the meaning of the demonstrative
pronouns "this" and "that" is not defined by the objects we
perceive but by the point of view of the observer, that is, by the
relationship to the objects. We could reverse the sequence of
the two pronouns in this sentence. Similarly, we do not *see*
"bigger"; rather, "bigger" is a "judgment" based on comparing
the trees in our mind. We can arrive at this judgment just as
"simply and directly" as we can see the trees, without thinking,
because the concepts are already instilled into our senses. Even
the way we see trees, therefore, is determined by concepts, for
without the "concept" tree—taken here in the nominalistic
sense—we would see only branches, trunks, and leaves. If we
did not have these concepts either, we would probably see
merely shapes or differently colored spots. Nevertheless, even
these distinctions, when made by *thinking* consciousness, are
based on concepts. If we stripped perception of all concepts,
no discrete particulars and no distinctions would remain. We
have less difficulty realizing that other relationships, for
example, those of cause and effect, are by nature conceptual
and not perceptible.

Neither discrete particulars nor the relationships between
them are *isolated*; in fact, we cannot even conceive them as
isolated. For example, we cannot think of "sun" without also
thinking of sky and of the sun's path through it, of light, dark,

day, night, morning, noon, and succession in time. The same is true for relationships: "that" goes with "this," "below" with "above," "next to" with "right" and "left," and so on. What is more, the particulars and their relationships are dependent upon each other. For instance, in an area where mechanical causality is the general explanatory principle, it makes no sense to speak of "kindness" or "friendship," or even of "cognizing" and "understanding."

Moreover, the structuring of the given reveals that it consists ultimately of connections and relationships that must be grasped at the "junctions" where they intersect. These "junctions" are our concepts. On the one hand, our concepts must have clear boundaries to keep them from blending into each other; on the other, their boundaries must not be too hard, rigid, or impermeable, otherwise the transitions and connections between the concepts will be lost. Discrete particulars and relationships form a *discontinuous* structure; otherwise we would be unable to distinguish between them. At the same time, however, these discontinuities are also mutually interconnected and interdependent.

As adults, the structure of the given we perceive is determined by the course of our lives up to the moment when we first begin to reflect upon the given—that is, by our education, our upbringing, and our family. All these formative influences are based on our ability to speak and can be traced back to it. Hence a person's *mother tongue* is the basis for all subsequent structuring of the perceptual world.

The Pedagogy of Language

The first structuring of the given through concepts and conceptual understanding is given to children by the mother tongue—

not only by the spoken language but also by the expressive, "speaking" behavior of the adult environment, behind which lies the adults' ability to speak and to grasp the world and situations conceptually. Except for a few exceptional situations, human beings continuously *communicate* through gestures, mimicry, looks, and movements.

Behind audible, spoken language and "speaking" behavior lies hidden the powerful concealed aspect of language, namely, the *speech intention*. Without this speech intention, which corresponds to the listener's *understanding*, speech does not normally happen. When a child learns to speak, this "immaterial" reality (understanding) is *directly* accessible. If it were not, the child could not understand what was heard. Language is unique in that it is not just perception but *meaningful* perception. Children must grasp both perception and meaning *at the same time*. This is the source of the consciousness functions of perceiving and thinking, which are later separated.

This characterization of the first structure of the given clearly shows the qualities of language. Language has an outer side that appears to be discontinuous and that corresponds to the particulars in the structure of the given. The inner side of language—understanding—connects and understands these discontinuities; it is related to the connections and relationships between particulars and indeed is the source of these relationships and connections.

The discontinuous structuring, as well as the perceptual and conceptual structuring of the given, is given in advance by the *phenomenon of language*—not only in principle (in that one part of it is perceptible while the other is hidden from our senses and remains an inner act of our consciousness) but also as the concrete structure of the two parts. Language structures our consciousness, our thinking, and thus also our perceiving. Language prefigures the union of perception and understanding;

it exemplifies at once their separation and their reunion in being "read together."

Thus, the first structure of the given is modeled on the pattern and inner structure of our mother tongue. Therefore, thinking at first can vary widely in style in accordance with the almost unimaginable variety of language patterns. Even among European languages, grammatical categories have only a very limited applicability. Two sentences that are very similarly constructed in one language can be completely unlike each other in another language. Thus the way we think, the "logic" of our languages, and the amount and extent of abstractions and concretization differ widely. Today, these differences are almost completely hidden, not only because those who dominate contemporary civilization use an Indo-European language, and because the way of thinking of these languages has spread over most of the world, but also because our thinking has largely emancipated itself from language.[29]

We perceive ourselves as subjects through inner experiences, especially through the experience of thinking. Like the experience of our ability to speak, these inner experiences are super-conscious. They are colored and influenced by the way we experience our body. The processes of thought, however, are also shaped by the pattern of our language, which determines both the separation of subject and object and the consequent integration of the subject into the world in the act of cognition. In fact, the mother tongue even influences the way the I takes possession of the body and begins to express itself through it.

After all, speaking is also the result of a physiological effort of the speech organs, which are part of our system of movement. The movements of our speech organs are determined by the sound structure of our language, and since movements are

---

29. See Kühlewind, *Das Licht des Wortes*, chapter entitled "Das wortlose Denken."

always executed by our entire being, by our whole system of movement, language thus influences our whole being and its movements. English-speaking people, for instance, not only move their mouth and face differently from French-speaking people, but all their movements and their whole body posture are different. Our system of movement connects the I with the rest of the organism; therefore, this connection occurs predominantly through our learning to speak.

Thus, the way we develop our basic human faculties shapes our experience and perception of our own body. The *how* of our movements of limbs, eyes, and facial muscles—whether these movements are intentional or in imitation of others—is as superconscious as the "how" of our speaking and thinking. In fact, all three faculties are closely connected and are also linked to our upright posture.

The use of language is often compared to a game—a "language-game"—and we can extend this analogy to thinking. However, there is a very significant difference between such language games and all other games in that we do not have to learn the rules of speaking and thinking; in fact, these rules are not even explicitly known. Instead, we acquire them as superconscious faculties. In all other games the rules must be learned before we can play. Through these two special "games" of thinking and perceiving, the world is given to us as a mass of discontinuities; and thereby also we are the only beings who have a world, a picture of the world—precisely *because* we perceive the discontinuities as structured. Without the structuring effect of concepts, which is based on the discontinuous structure of language, we would not find any discontinuities in the world as such. Through concepts determined by language—that is, word-concepts—we gradually make our thinking independent of language and develop concepts that transcend language. This is the precondition for a style of thinking that is valid and

attainable for all people and that will make connections possible
that are valid and identical for everyone.

The basis of human freedom is the activity of *reading*
between two givens—perceptions and concepts—because the
activity by which these two are "read together" is *not* given.
Consequently, for the cognizing subject, freedom exists only
in *new* cognitions, for what we have already cognized and
understood must be considered part of the given.

The First Structuring of the Given

Today, the given inner world and the outer perceptual world
are full of riddles; they pose questions and call for an understanding that is not given. These questions, themselves conceptual forms, anticipate conceptual, ideal answers. The given
is questionable for us as questioners, and as we have seen,
questioning carries its own conditions.

We have referred to the two separated levels of consciousness between which consciousness can oscillate, with the
result that consciousness takes two looks at the given. The second look reveals that existing concepts do not suffice to make
the given comprehensible. We will later see that this same
structure of our consciousness makes possible the emancipation of our conceptual thinking from language. The transition
to a questioning consciousness and to the questionableness of
the given required a long process of development—whose
results appeared only recently, relatively late in human history,
in the sciences, which are based on questions. This means that
the first form of the given was *not* questionable. Profound
changes had to occur in the given as well as in our consciousness—on which the given is partly contingent—before we
could reach the level we have reached today.

Concepts structure the directly given into particulars and connections. Concepts themselves are not discrete units but always emerge within systems of concepts or relationships. The first system of this kind is given by the mother tongue. The resulting first structuring of the given is not at all questionable because it is *complete*. In other words, concepts completely and seamlessly structure the perceptual given—nothing else exists yet—into discrete particulars, without leaving any gaps not covered by concepts.

Let us use an analogy to understand this better. For example, imagine a surface subdivided into small parts, so that the parts cover the whole surface without leaving any gaps. Concepts structure (articulate) particulars *out* of the given continuum while at the same time structuring them back (reintegrating them) *into* the unified field of perception. Thereby a complete transition between "structuring out" (distinction) and "structuring in" (reintegration) is possible, indeed is the only possibility.

At first, structuring of this kind develops in the two directions at once because our intellect, which distinguishes particulars, and our reason, which reunites them, are still united. As yet, there is also no inner world; rather, our attention is completely oriented in *one* direction, which *today* we call the outer world. We will discuss in chapter 4 how we are to think these "concepts," how they simultaneously structure the given *and* make it comprehensible.

In the first form of the given, then, questions are not only impossible—because we are not yet able to distance ourselves from the structured whole of the world—but also unnecessary because in that stage the world is whole and complete and consists only of particulars that "explain" each other seamlessly without leaving any gaps. The system of concepts provided by language structures the unified, given perceptual world. The only concepts we know are those our language gives us. The systems of speaking and thinking are one and the same; in Humboldt's words, we are in the "energetic" phase of language development. In this phase languages do not simply label something that already exists; rather they demarcate and define the "somethings." Concepts indicate where "something" ends, where its boundary is, for "in the given there actually are no discrete entities, but everything is in continuous connection."[30] This statement obviously refers to the "directly given."

The epoch or stage of consciousness described above may also be called the epoch of the *magic* word. On the one hand, there was no separation or distinction between word, concept, and "thing;" on the other, people still experienced the word in its living occurrence, in its "arriving"—and not only in its immobilized and finished form on the consciousness level of the past. Communication between I-beings through speech or speech-song was then an immediate and spiritual interaction. For instance, in the *Kalevala* (Song III), the battle between Väjnemöjnen and Joukahajnen, a direct test of the power of the I, is fought through singing. The weaker of the two must yield to the power of the words of the stronger; they force him into the course of events they foretell or dictate.

If the first system of concepts structuring the world is given to us by our language, then the way this structure is built can differ widely because our languages are structured very differently. This may also be observed. Some languages, such as German, are flectional; that is, they use inflections. Others, such as ancient Chinese, are isolating; that is, they use neither declensions, conjugations, prepositions, nor suffixes; neither changes in the stem of words nor separate classes of words,

---

30. . See Steiner, *Truth and Knowledge* (GA 3), chapter 5.

such as nouns, verbs, and adjectives. Instead, in such isolating languages, the roots of words are simply strung in a sequence. The proportion of the perceptible part of the language to the hidden part differs in these two types of languages. Isolating languages generally have fewer words and require much more inner activity to complement the vocal, audible part of the language than European languages. Some languages consist entirely of "verbs," for example, that of the Nootka Eskimos—that is, they contain only words we would classify as "verbs" in the European languages. In those languages everything, even what we would express in nouns, is occurrence or process. Roughly two-thirds of the known languages do not conjugate verbs to form tenses; they structure time differently than we do. In these languages time is not the same idea it is for us.

The outer and inner sides of languages differ enormously, for example, the poly-synthetic languages of the American Indians or Eskimos, with their giant words, which often have to be translated as long sentences in a European language, are totally different from an analytic language, such as French. As linguists have long known, language shapes our thinking and thus the structure of the world in the first phase of consciousness. Nevertheless, the outer and inner sides of every language complement each other so that nothing is missing from any language; there is nothing that cannot be expressed in any language.

For example, many languages do not assign a gender to their nouns, or they do it differently than, for example, German; they may have more or fewer "genders" than German. Such "defects" go unnoticed because they are not really shortcomings. Whether it is easy or difficult to express something depends on the topic and on the language. For instance, it is easier to discuss dialectical philosophy in German than in the Hopi language; talking about elementary spiritual truths concerning nature and human beings is probably easier in the Hopi language.

The two complementary parts of language, the perceptible one and the hidden one, combine to make a whole that is common to all languages. This language-of-understanding is the shared property of all humanity. It allows us to understand one another across linguistic boundaries and makes translation—despite its limitations—possible. Still, understanding one another is easier than translating. This shared property of all humanity is the realm of higher thinking, a thinking that transcends language.

The differences in the structure of the various languages result in differences in the structure of the world. Accordingly, the first given picture of the world is different in each language. For example, many languages subdivide the color spectrum differently than we do in English. Similarly, the entire inner and outer world is structured differently from one language to the next. In other words, a certain *relativity* appears in the given pictures of the world: the particulars and their connections vary with the language.[31]

Clearly, the first given picture of the world—the one that precedes scientific inquiry and is not based on questioning—does not show us the whole of reality because it is contingent on our language. We can reach this full and complete reality only by overcoming the thinking conditioned by language. This is made possible by the structure of the consciousness soul, and by conscious cognitive activity based on questions.

These thoughts and observations lead to the following. On the one hand, our "organization," which determines the given, consists of the physical foundation of our senses and our

---

31. Rudolf Steiner has repeatedly alluded to this; see, for example, his *Philosophy of Freedom* (GA 4), chapter 7.

thinking, which we inherit and have at our disposal when we are born. On the other hand, this organization is also made up of the "schooling" of the increasing free forces that make our specifically human faculties possible. These faculties are not inherited—a fact that the sciences have not properly taken into account. Regardless of their country of origin, children can learn any language as their mother tongue. In this earliest "schooling" of the human faculties, language—or rather speaking—is all-important, for it largely determines our early organization.

4. The Language of Reality

....

*T*he idea of reality, like the idea of cognition, can emerge only in the questioning individual. Various ideas can be associated with the word "reality," but for modern human beings it inevitably refers to a particular *sensation* that categorically asserts that something is *real*. From this it follows—and we can easily experience this—that there are also other "givens" that do not evoke this sensation and are therefore *not* real. But if they do not have the quality of "reality," what quality do they have? For modern thinkers this is an idle question.

It would be overhasty to identify the sensation of reality with that of tangibility; after all, we have this sensation with many things that are not tangible, such as sounds, smells, warmth, and so on. We do not often test whether what we see is real by touching it. By the same token, we all acknowledge force fields—such as in the economy, the state, or our feelings—that often have greater power over us than anything tangible and that are effective, that is, real. However, in the natural sciences as well as in our thinking we transfer these "realities" into the world of tangibility, which we believe to be identical with the perceptual world. In fact, this sensation of reality does derive from the perceptual world. We will look at this further in more detail in chapter 5.

We "experience" certain elements of consciousness, for example, thoughts and concepts, without having this sensation of reality. Obviously, then, "sensed" reality does not appear "real" because of its conceptual nature. Rather, this sensation of reality must be ascribed to the nonconceptual part of perception. However, this applies only to human beings today, and it would be wrong to assume that people had similar perceptions and sensations in the "energetic" phase of language consciousness. Similarly, we cannot speak of "truth" in the modern sense when we talk about this archaic consciousness. "Truth"—in relation to the perceptual world—would be the adequate conceptual insight into the nature of the perceptual world. This insight itself—that is, the truth—does not evoke the sensation of reality; instead, it is accompanied by what we can call a feeling of *evidence*.

This feeling of evidence or obviousness also characterizes purely conceptual judgments. We consider them *true* when they are "right" and when they "agree," not with a phenomenon of the perceptual world, but with themselves, so that they evoke the feeling of "self-evidence" and thereby satisfy the thinker. Truth or evidence as such cannot be defined. In fact, they cannot even be described because every statement we make about them would have to be identified and felt as true or evident to be acceptable and conceivable. All reductionist theories that try to reduce cognition or understanding to noncognitive or nonunderstanding processes cancel themselves out, as we have shown in chapter 1.

When, meditatively, we penetrate below the surface of the given, we experience that concepts control everything we perceive, insofar as what we perceive is a THAT, something we can point to, something that is defined and outlined. As we have seen also, in the first structuring of the given, everything without exception is conceptual: nothing remains conceptually unpenetrated. Therefore, this first form of the given is not questionable; concepts cover the given completely, without any gaps. If we in modern consciousness could attain such a complete conceptual covering, truth and reality would merge and become one. We do not know whether this was the case for people in archaic times, because they had neither the concept of "reality" nor that of "truth." They lived in the *true reality* without looking for it or questioning it. People question and search for true reality only when they have lost it. People in those early times did not need a synthesis of percept and concept because for them they were still united. We, however, experience them as given separately. (The story of how this true reality was lost will follow later.)

Today the above-mentioned two feelings—the sensation of reality and the experience of evidence—determine what is true and real. Nevertheless, it is conceivable that thinking and perceiving could come together in a human, conscious synthesis and form a true or full reality.[32]

The two feelings would then interpenetrate, and the feeling for reality would be illumined—which it usually is not—while the feeling of evidence would no longer remain abstract but be filled with warmth and life and become a concrete perception. In other words, full reality would emerge from the interpenetration of a perception and its—adequate—concept. Then no questions would remain, and the desire for knowledge would be satisfied. Without this interpenetration of percept and concept, the given remains questionable; that is, it needs to be completed. With regard to the reality we perceive, neither the given percept nor the concept by itself constitutes the full reality. Neither the original union of these two elements in archaic consciousness—where the concepts of language structure the perceptual world—nor their new synthesis is *additive*. Rather, both the concept and the perceptual element undergo a qualitative change when they interpenetrate—something we can experience daily, if we pay attention.

---

32. See Steiner, *Truth and Knowledge* (GA 3), Preface, and *The Philosophy of Freedom* (GA 4), chapter entitled "The Consequences of Monism."

The First Reality — The First Language

The first, full reality is wholly given to us in the union of the percept with an adequate concept, which made the percept into *this* percept. We can hardly overlook that this first reality is related to the state of the world and the human being that many traditions have described, under various names, as paradise. According to all authentic traditions, human beings were already endowed with the gift of language. That mythologies do not speak about "reality" is only natural for a state of consciousness where questions were nonexistent. Perhaps our image of paradise—at least in regard to the absence of questioning—is only a rather radical projection onto the past of an extreme condition, one whose image was designed along the lines of an increasingly "obscured" consciousness.

There are good reasons to believe that today the world is never unquestionable for children in any phase of the process of their learning to speak. Children experience words more deeply than the adults from whom they learn. For instance, for adults the designations of natural objects are hardly more than mere names (see chapter 2, "Reflecting on Concepts"). When adults say these names, they are therefore no longer accompanied by an inner understanding. Thus the children, likewise, can no longer experience this understanding. In contrast, adults fully understand what the word "but" means, even though most would probably have a hard time explaining it. Still, since we understand this word, its meaning is also accessible to children by direct insight into what they hear. When the children hear adults talk about "horses" or "pines," however, they do not find such an inner understanding.

Language has handed down words to us that we now understand only in a nominalistic sense. However, there are three reasons why we should not assume that, even originally, these words were only arbitrary names to label a phenomenon or object. First, as we have seen, the concepts of our language initially structure the perceptual world—and *only through these concepts* can we perceive its particulars. Second, we can name only things that have already been conceptually defined and outlined. Since we receive our first concepts through language, any "naming" is superfluous. Third, ethnological studies show that human activity has *never* produced a *new* word stem.

When we encounter something new, we use old words or stems of words, though perhaps in a modified form, to name or describe the new experience. For instance, the Navajo Indians describe what we call film or movie in a phrase that means "those who are gliding past one after the other." They call elephants, for which there is, of course, no original word in their language, "the one who throws a lasso with his nose" (free translation). Indeed, even in modern European languages we use old words for new inventions, or we use compound words, such as "television," or we adopt words from other languages.

In short, there is no known case of a new word stem being created—not even in modern times and not counting, of course, words derived from old roots, for example, through contraction. Thus, all terms for natural objects, which are mere names for us today, were in their original or ancient form (all words have gone through changes) as meaningful as words like "spoon" or "or" are for us now.

The old word-concepts of natural objects, then, were "understood." The structure of the archaic consciousness meant that people experienced the living, sentient higher concepts—which cannot be brought down to the plane of the past of modern consciousness—in a dreamlike way. Moreover, archaic perception was hardly, if at all, separate from "thinking" and could therefore grasp much more of nature than ours. In the structure of the archaic consciousness—and also in very young children in our time—the plane of the past is not yet separated from that of the present by an abyss. For this reason it has a more dreamlike character and lacks sharp distinctions. It is linked, as if by resonance, with the continuity of the upper levels of consciousness, which for us are now in the *superconscious*. Words or word-concepts in this archaic consciousness still carry within them a far-reaching perceptive feeling and willing by means of which the "concept"—very different from what we know as concepts—sends its roots deep into the perceptual world, touching the creational ideas of nature. These word-concepts are connections—*relationships*—in the perceptual world and structure it. They do not name "objects" but rather are relationships between what later separates into subject and object.

The I-being still lives in a unified world, in understanding. It experiences the world and itself as understanding, in a harmony—the later music of the spheres is a pale reflection of this—that is a sign of "understanding" what the natural world, the cosmos, is "saying." It is an understanding from within, without juxtaposition and without any I-consciousness. The great ideas of nature are experienced in communion, and initially the human being is one of these ideas. In the archaic languages every word is an aspect of the world that structures the world while at the same time reintegrating into a unity the particulars that are distinguished.

Words that designated objects in nature were then not just names; they were even more than true universals. A species, for example, a "red maple," was experienced as more real than the individual tree. In contrast, for us "maple" is now the name of the individual tree, and using the word for the species seems to us an abstraction. It was the same with designations of natural objects in fairy tales and myths. In fact, even in the Old Testament, the name of a people is a reality; "Amalek," for instance, is not a comprehensive or general term but an idea that gives the members of a people their character. Moreover, "maple" (or the corresponding original word) also signified a function, a relationship to earth and sky, to other trees, to the air, and also to human beings. It designated a "character" that had a value for feeling and willing and also still other qualities unknown to us that still "spoke" to archaic consciousness, linking human beings in consciousness with nature.

To characterize archaic consciousness today we have to describe it alternately in its two aspects of perception and thinking because we *now* experience these two functions separately. But the essence of archaic consciousness is that these two functions are still united, and representational mental pictures are thus not subject to human whim. If "thinking" is alive, colorful, warm, saturated with feeling, and pulsating, then "perceiving" is transilluminated within itself by the ideal or ideating "thinking" that indwells it and not by any instruction; "perceiving" then is already structuring everything out and reading everything together, including the beings of nature known in every tradition. If nature still speaks to human beings, its speaking must come from beings who are themselves I-beings or who represent I-beings—if the latter have already withdrawn from their work. The structure of the archaic senses will be outlined in chapter 5.

In his theory of knowledge, Rudolf Steiner alludes to the possibility that percept and concept are already united in the given. This, indeed, is true for the first, entirely given image of reality in the first phase of language development. "Were there a totality, complete in itself, in the directly given, then it would be impossible, as well as unnecessary, to elaborate it [by thinking] in the process of cognition. Rather, we would simply accept the given as it is and would be satisfied with it in that form.... If, in the world-content, the thought-content were united with the given from the outset, no cognition would exist."[33]

Following our discussion above, we have to rephrase this sentence as follows: If, in the world-content, the content of our thoughts were from the outset united with the content of our perception, there would be no humanly elaborated cognition. For in chapter 6 of *Truth and Knowledge*, Steiner speaks of cognition as a "still unconscious activity of the I" that must be raised to consciousness by the theory of knowledge. In *The Philosophy of Freedom* Steiner writes: "It would indeed be quite possible for a mind to receive the concept simultaneously with the percept and not separated from the latter. Such a mind would never consider the concept as something separate from the object but would ascribe to the concept an existence indivisibly bound up with the object."[34] Archaic thought life is often described by Steiner as a "complete givenness."[35]

The first reality is given, but given to *human beings*, for in the world the gods have created, the human is the only being through whom ideality, word, and concept as such can emerge and flourish. The Logos-world attains its first reality in the only Logos-being of *this* world.

Our contribution to producing the *first* reality is entirely passive; idea and percept are already united when they appear in consciousness. Language not only participates in the configuration of the given, it cannot be separated from the given reality. Therefore, it is trivial to say that reality is structured like language; the two sides of language are disguised as percept and concept. The inner changes in language gradually guide archaic consciousness into a questioning one; that is, they lead it to the second reality, the second language.

33. See Steiner, *Truth and Knowledge* (GA 3), chapter 5, pp. 69, 70.
34. See Steiner, *The Philosophy of Freedom* (GA 4), chapter 5, pp.76, 80.
35. Rudolf Steiner, (GA 212, lectures of May 27 and June 17, 1922).

The Transition to Questioning

Different languages lift different conceptual systems out of the unstructured continuum of the directly given. These conceptual systems exist in the continuum not in a preformed state but as "potential." Percepts and concepts, initially seamlessly congruent, manifest in human beings. This means that human cognitive activity—whether conscious or not—must be considered part of reality. In archaic consciousness this activity was not experienced as separate from its result, which is the image of reality. In chapter 5 we will discuss why we now do not *experience* our cognitive activity as part of reality.

Due to profound changes in human consciousness, the first reality has been lost. It is difficult to describe the reasons and motivating forces behind these changes without using the language of myths. In the Old Testament the changes are described as the events of the Fall. The changes have cut us off from nature and from the spiritual beings who inspire and guide us. As a result, we have become capable of erring and sinning, and now, in the era of the consciousness soul, we have to choose our further path as mature, emancipated beings.

This long process is reflected in the changes in our languages, which have always possessed the potential for this development. Language's twofoldness prefigures every other dualism, particularly the division of perceiving and thinking. The discontinuous structure of the outer aspect of language bears the seed for all further atomization. By the same token, the hidden part of language contains the image and potential for all unifying and synthesizing, for all "reading together." The duality of perception and the inner act that complements it—present in language—continues into the duality of object and subject. Today it is possible to realize that *understanding* and *what is understood*—the planes of the present and the past in our consciousness—form the basic dual structure of the consciousness soul which makes it possible for consciousness to reflect upon itself.

The outer changes, which we shall consider first, are not limited to a particular language but affect the whole range of languages, including those usually classified as archaic or primitive, as developed or highly flectional languages. This range of languages is often mistakenly considered to consist of developmental stages. As far as the original store of word stems and grammatical structures is concerned, we can find losses and signs of deterioration within *any* particular language. However, the emancipation of thinking makes every language more complicated insofar as it creates more complicated associations between thoughts in newly opened areas of world and consciousness.

If one compares archaic languages with more "developed" ones, one notices that, as the latter increase both their vocabulary and their sense-perceptible part, their perceptual picture—as well as their whole picture of the world—loses more and more of the unity it had in the archaic languages. Increasingly, terms for connections become mere names for things; and the connections themselves are expressed more and more in the perceptible part of the language, for example, through inflections, prefixes, suffixes, prepositions, and syntactical rules. The real, higher relationships, connections, and concepts, however, cannot *appear*; they remain completely in the hidden part of the language.

The more a language appears sense-perceptible, the less inner work is necessary to complement it. As a result, the perceptible part is less permeated with life and feeling. Ultimately, language then ends up a mere carrier of information, and the duality of "sign and meaning" develops accordingly. In other words, this duality becomes even more pronounced as thinking emancipates itself from language. What do we have "information" about? About the world, which was first given through language in its energetic phase and which we then made from out of this primary reality.

As the multitude of particulars grows in the development of language, the connections dwindle away. This development is also reflected by changes in vocabulary; for instance, archaic languages are rich in verbs, and the predominance of predicates gives these languages their distinctive character. In more modern languages, however, nouns and adjectives predominate.

In addition to these "external" changes there are also important developments in the hidden part of each language. Words that were still fluid in earlier times and expressed connections now dry up and shrink more and more to mere names of particulars. Thus, the particular becomes questionable, not in regard to the universality of concepts, but rather in its disconnectedness and in the quality of its being.

When the connections vanish from the nouns, and consciousness experiences in the sound of a word only what was separated out without its simultaneous reintegration, then the question concerning the *how* becomes urgent. Thinking begins to search for connections, for principles that link the particulars, outside the sphere given by language. At first, we retain the structure of the perceptual world through the word-concepts of language, but the concepts gradually become mere shells of words, and the connections dwindle away. We have to find them again through new concepts independent of language.

The above-mentioned analogy of the subdivided surface may be used again to describe this new situation. The small pieces now no longer extend over the whole surface completely. Instead, the concepts have shrunk to the size of points; that is, they have become entirely nominal. The remaining, uncovered parts of the surface thus leave ample room, and provide compelling reasons, for asking questions—about the perceptual world or about the relationships between the point-like concepts.

The human being now adds the concepts connecting the percepts to the latter. Generally, we are not aware that the perceptual world is already structured through the remnants of the language-concepts before we add new concepts to it. In any case, whether in the first phase of consciousness or later, reality is always created through the union of percept and concept. Initially, this union was given; later, human beings themselves had to bring about the synthesis. The joining of percept and concept does not permit any arbitrariness; although we are the ones bringing together and uniting the elements of reality—namely, the structured percept and the concept—we do so in accordance with *their* own nature. We wait to see what emerges from the union of these elements. The faculty of forming concepts is becoming more and more individualized, and in time it is less and less formed by the mother tongue—the "folk-spirit"—or by cultural styles that transcend language, such as the baroque style—the "spirit of the times."

The concepts provided by language were much more than mere connections; they were felt, living, willing, and experienced realities.

The development of consciousness inherent in the pedagogy of language—every language guides the people speaking it to a particular configuration of consciousness—can cause word-concepts to lose their life and become mere names of things outside themselves (except for conjunctions, such as "although"). This leaves two paths open to us, both of which have become possible only because of the new capacity to think independently of language.

One path leads to *logical*, abstract concepts, which can be reduced to a common denominator, so to speak, through the word-concepts of various languages, and therefore can be translated. The *logical* concepts of "water," "*eau*," "*aqua*," and "hydro" are equivalent, and the words are interchangeable in this regard. Such words, however, differ in mood and character and also in the ways in which they can be applied and connected to others in their respective languages. This is especially obvious in translations of poetry. Structuralism calls this phenomenon the *valence* or *value* of words. We derive the logical concept through abstraction from the different values of the words; thus, logical concepts transcend language. Accordingly, they rank below word-concepts because they are poorer. When thinkers begin to realize this, they resort to language—for instance, to etymology—to enrich the abstract logical concepts, to understand them better, and to awaken them to life.

But there is another path. Rising above the word-concepts we can reach the meditative or creational concepts. These contain all word-concepts and integrate them. Such meditative concepts are therefore richer than word-concepts. They enable word-concepts to unite in the logical concepts—this impoverished union is, so to speak, their abstract reflection directed downward. The creational concepts were already abstract by the Middle Ages; they were no longer experienced but only grasped as thought intuitions.[36] As such, they were called *universalia ante rem.**

From this point of view, one could identify logical concepts as *universalia post rem*;** however, the third kind of universal has no parallel in modern consciousness.***

---

36. See also Steiner, *Die geistige Vereinigung der Menschheit durch den Christus-Impuls* (GA 165) (Dornach, Switzerland: Rudolf Steiner Verlag, 1981), lecture of January 15,1916.

*"Universals" before their embodiment in matter. Translator's note.

**"Universals," understood *after* being experienced in their embodied reality. Translator's note.

****"Universalia in re,"* "universals" as the functional idea according to which a thing is given its conceptual definition *while it is in use.* Translator's note.

For example, "human being," "*anthropos*," and "*homo*" obviously have different valences or aspects. The logical concept of these words is formed by the outer, perhaps physiological, characteristics of the human being, but the creational concept comprises the Word- or Logos-character of human nature, its indwelling archetype, potential, freedom, and relationship to the whole cosmos as *one* idea. Obviously, this idea requires a consciousness that rises far above everyday consciousness. Judging by the sound alone, we do not perceive a connection between the words "rose," "*varda*," and "*gul*." However, we can perhaps glimpse their common creational idea behind the idea of the white rose in Dante's *Paradiso* (Par. 31. and 32.), which is the "Throne of the Blessed."

Western science has taken the first path mentioned above, the one leading to logical concepts. In the process everything else has been excluded. The consequences of this choice urge us now to try out the other path to balance and heal our one-sidedness.

The Second Reality

When the first given reality fades, we retain only its remnants and ruins. Now we have to strive to put together the "patchwork" by ourselves. The patchwork is already interwoven with concepts, but they do not form a seamless network. As a result, the world has become open to question, questionable. At the same time, language has taught us the secret of structured thinking and perceiving. We now try to find suitable concepts to understand the questionable world independent of our teacher, language. We want to reintegrate what has been separated out of the continuum.

We strive to penetrate the given completely with understanding and conceptuality[37] in order to bring the feeling of reality into coincidence with the feeling of truth: we seek the "full" or "true" reality. In other words, it is *we* who are now creating reality, because we are no longer satisfied with the feeling or sensation of reality—at least not in regard to the perceptual world.

The relativity of the first reality was due to the mother tongue; the second reality, however, is structured through the new concepts, conceived independently of language. This in turn relativizes the synthesis of the perceptual with the conceptual aspect of reality, but at the same time "reality" and "truth" become dynamic ideas capable of further development. Perceptual reality and pure thinking are given space to play. Our striving for knowledge does not gravitate toward any predetermined, absolute truth and reality; rather, we have the possibility of progressing from "unconcealedness" (*aletheia*, the Greek word for truth) to unconcealedness, from light to brighter light, from idea to idea. We contribute to the creation of the world.

Every cognition changes us, and since we are part of reality, reality too is continuously being transformed. We create future reality—not just in the sense of future time, but in the essential sense of new beginnings. As I-beings capable of making beginnings and taking initiatives, we can sow seeds for the future. Thus, we can describe freedom as unconditioned, as the ability to make new beginnings that are not contingent on, and do not follow necessarily from, existing reality. As we have seen, cognition itself is such a beginning.

The human contribution to the given is already concealed within the given, but it is not fully preformed. Otherwise cognition would be a merely formal, and not a creative,

---

37. See Steiner, *Truth and Knowledge* (GA 3, p. 65), p. 70; *The Philosophy of Freedom* (GA 4, pp. 112, 115, 247-248), pp. 100, 102-103, 235-236.

activity that adds something new to the reality that already
"is." In other words, cognition is itself reality.[38]

In the first reality, guided by our mother tongue, we structure and connect the given; in the second reality, we follow the
concepts we have now intuited independently of language.
The potential reality, slumbering concealed within the given, is
always actualized by human cognitive activity; it is production, not reproduction.

The new structure of consciousness, which enables us to
question, is based on the complete separation of the planes of
consciousness of the past and of the present, of thought and of
thinking. As a result, the latter has moved into the superconscious sphere. We can now turn and ask questions in both
directions; in fact, this is the mission of the consciousness
soul. However, our gaze does not turn equally and impartially
in both directions; the upper plane is entirely hidden from our
inner eye (see chapter 8). We do not see it. At first, we do not
investigate the lower plane either, because, being on the plane
of the past, it does not evoke the sensation of reality. For this
reason, we experience the perceptual world, or nature, as all
the more real. This explains why, historically, human questions
were at first wholly related to nature.

Historically, questions about consciousness only arise when
the "natural scientific" way of formulating questions ("what is
it made of?" and "how?") becomes so deeply rooted that a different style of questioning—appropriate to problems of consciousness—becomes impossible. This predominance of one
style of questioning also influences the concepts that are to
penetrate natural phenomena. These new concepts have two

---

38. See Steiner, *A Theory of Knowledge* (GA 2, pp. 136-137), pp. 120-121; *Truth
and Knowledge* (GA 3, p. 11), p.11 and *The Fruits of Anthroposophy* (GA 78, pp.
27, 31, 32), (Hudson, N.Y.: Anthroposophic Press, 1986), lecture of August 30,
1921, summarized pp. 8-1).

distinctive features: first, they are contingent only upon a part, a partial aspect, of the given—for example, the concepts of mechanics are contingent on the aspect of lifelessness. Second, the connecting principles or explanatory concepts are of the same type as the concepts they are intended to connect. Again, this is typical of mechanics; its explanatory principles do not *read* reality because the conceptual structure is no longer adequate to the perceptual picture. As a result, part of the perceptual picture remains nonconceptual and therefore not transparent to the understanding.

The general application of the mechanistic style of thinking and the predominance of mechanical causality arise from the subconscious; they cannot be logically justified. Modern thinkers know of hardly any connections or causes except mechanical ones. Aristotle was still aware of others, for example, the *causa exemplaris*, that of the model or example.

Because mechanical connections, as explanatory principles between things, are on the same level as the things themselves, they are *effective* and even *compelling*, for instance, gravitation as the relationship between apple and earth. However, when the explanatory principle remains on the same level as the phenomenon to be explained, as in this case, the resulting explanation never represents true *understanding* as does the full understanding of a thought in which there remains no further questions about the statement; when no understanding is reached, or only a limited understanding, we can continue to question until we arrive at a *pure* thought—as is the usual procedure in mathematics. However, in natural science we do this at the expense of the qualities, which are lost in this procedure.

Mechanics and mechanistic thinking are on a level below the sense-perceptible simply because they seek to reduce all qualities to entities without qualities, to particles and forces. While the older worldview was concerned with the purpose, direction, and meaning of phenomena—with their "why," their motivation—mechanistic thinking focuses only on the "hard" facts, their application, and their "how," that is, their mechanism. For example, Galileo reduced all qualities to those of size, shape, number, and movement. Then he explained these "qualities"—if they can still be called such—by the concepts of force, resistance, and velocity. These concepts were borrowed and adapted from the living world; but there they have an *intentional* character. Ancient science was a science of essence, whereas modern science deals with mechanisms and transformations.

Describing processes mathematically is not the same as *understanding* them. For a mathematical description we first observe a natural process (or reconstruct its assumed course) using a model of it as a guideline, then we describe what we have observed in symbols and mathematical equations. By now we have taken two steps uncritically and even without noticing it. First, "cognition" has already determined *what* we have to describe mathematically, but we have not questioned this "what" epistemologically (i.e., in terms of a theory of cognition). Second, we use symbols in our mathematical description, such as those for mass, density, velocity, and so on, even though we have not examined or ascertained them epistemologically either. Thus, "successful" mathematical descriptions often attribute concreteness to entities that do not originate in our observation of the given perceptual world—the entities gain concreteness or have concreteness ascribed to them by the "success" of the mathematical description. Such entities are often part of our presuppositions when we formulate the model or hypothesis; and later on we are inclined to consider them more real than the perceptions we started with.

For more or less unhealthy thinking the usual questions about reality focus on two points. The first concerns the world of thought: Are our ideas and concepts already fully formed in the superconscious sphere or in a spiritual world, where we simply "copy" them, or do we ourselves form our concepts and ideas out of the world of ideas? The second point and question concerns the perceptual world: Are nature and its phenomena already "there," do they exist, before we cognize them?

Both questions bear the stamp of learned cognitive naïveté. Moreover, the first question originates in a misunderstood Platonism that assumes the "world of ideas" consists of *particular* finished, fully formed ideas, which we can then "bring down" as needed. In this regard we can learn much from studying a foreign language that is very different from our own. We will then vividly experience the relativity of conceptual systems. For instance, it seems logical to us to conjugate all verbs in the same way: I run, I stand, I sleep; you run, you stand, you sleep, and so on. However, a different type of "logic" would consider this conjugation completely illogical because it expresses very different facts in the same way. After all, running is an activity, so how could we treat standing or sleeping in the same way linguistically? We can exert ourselves in running—but in standing or sleeping? In fact, there are languages that take these differences into account, and accordingly they have different expressions for them.

The world of ideas does not consist of predetermined ideas because, if that were the case, their number would be limited. Rather, the world of ideas consists of the infinite *possibility*— corresponding to our *capacity*—to separate more and more ideas out of itself. This is what we do as soon as thinking has emancipated itself from language. If this were not the case, we could not even understand the differences between languages.

Concerning the second question, "nature" is indubitably not created by us and our cognitive processes. The real question is what we mean by "nature." What we call "nature" at a particular point in our development both as species and as individuals is already a *particular picture*, and we have participated, either consciously or unconsciously, in its creation. This is true both for the given perceptual picture and for the second, conscious cognitive understanding. Everything we *speak* about is always a picture that already contains our activity. To claim that, in this sense, nature has always existed would be naïve; this would imply that if people like us had faced the given reality of nature *before* we did, they would have seen the same picture of nature that we do, or at least a qualitatively similar one.

Seen as a text, however, nature is a letter we did not write—it would not be a riddle to us if we had written it—nor is it being written *now*, at this moment—the natural sciences would not be possible if it were. A text is always an interpreted text; it means what its reader understands. We are or could be readers of the letter that is nature. Our understanding is a reality, one that previously did not exist. For the moment, however, it is not yet clear *whether* nature is a text at all.

The given—nature, perceiving, thinking, attention, and so on—is *given,* without any present contribution on our part. This is the meaning of the term "given" in principle, in its extreme form, beyond any epistemology, i.e., without any structuring of the given. As soon as we have a *mental picture* of it, however, the given is structured; this is the stage of particulars. Neither this structure nor the *picture* of the given exist apart from us. After all, even human beings in their "givenness" are not their own creations. We only *become* our own creations; we become what we cognize ourselves to be (not what we imagine or fancy).

Thus, everything we speak or think about or we ask questions about is already a mental picture, a known element, a structure. This is the power and fundamental character of the word, of which we are normally unaware. After all, we cannot talk about something we do not know or cannot know, and when we try this anyway, we always bring what we already know into our thinking. The "thing-in-itself," the "unconscious," "matter without properties," elementary particles that can be infinitely subdivided—all these bear witness to the unsuccessful endeavor to think the unthinkable, the nonideal, the nonwordlike. Only what is wordlike exists in the world of the Logos. In spite of this fact, an enormous attempt is underway to introduce what is not wordlike into this world and thus to destroy it.

The given is what has always "been there"; it is the remnant of the first reality, or to use a religious expression, it is the gift of the gods. What we experience, perceive, think, know, imagine, and what we talk about does not exist apart from us and never did. This truth may sound trivial; nevertheless, it follows from the insight that cognition is not a mere reproducing, copying, translating, or repeating of something that already existed *prior* to the act of cognition. Part of reality appears within us, namely, the idea. However, it is difficult to distinguish between *true* or *full* reality and the given, especially the perceptual given, because a feeling of autonomous existence is undoubtedly a characteristic of this part of true reality (see chapter 5).

When we ask whether the violet, the moon, or the unicorn already existed before we knew them, our real, underlying question is whether the mental pictures, images, and syntheses of percepts and concepts already existed before we created them. The answer is clear. What "already existed" prior to our activity is the given; from out of this given we have separated our concepts and percepts and created a synthesis.

The Third Reality

The structure of true or full reality is similar to that of language; that is, percept and meaning are united from the beginning. As long as language is not used in an entirely mechanical way, it retains the character of the first reality. In other words, its perceptual aspect functions as a sign; it *means* something. As soon as the first reality is lost, however, this unity disintegrates into the separate functions of perception and thinking, which originated in language. Only in this way can we become independent, free beings; in the sphere of thinking we can find this independence.

The perceptual world is no longer a world of signs but becomes a world of objects, and thus becomes questionable and enigmatic to thinking. The perceptual world retains, however, its feeling of reality for us, and we are therefore inclined to believe it is the full and complete reality. We do not realize that this perceptual world is given to us already interwoven with concepts, albeit insufficient ones that do not cover the given completely; this is why to thinking it is a problem to be solved. The given that was given to us without questions already existed *before* our cognition *was there*, before our conscious act of cognition.

The second reality is necessarily unsatisfactory, notwithstanding the promises of technology—which is based on this image of reality—to solve all problems. On the one hand, this reality is unsatisfactory in part because we cannot find the creational ideas or functional concepts of phenomena in nature—they can be reached only on higher planes of consciousness. On the other hand, we cannot account satisfactorily for cognition and the cognizer if we do not focus our attention on the cognitive functions of consciousness *themselves* rather than on what is often taken for their *mechanism*. As spiritual science showed at the end of the last century, we as modern people *can* and, indeed, of necessity *must* turn our attention in this direction.[39] Spiritual science later also presented the details and methodology of this new direction of our attention,[40] but to this day people have hardly understood them and even less put them into practice. Nevertheless, there can be no doubt that we can reach true reality only by raising our consciousness in both the directions of our cognitive life—that is, by forming, in our "thinking," *living, feeling, and willing ideas* that enable us to perceive and *read* the perceptual world as a realm of signs. Then true reality will be realized through us, and will be our own. We will discuss the requirements and necessary skills for attaining this third picture of reality in chapters 8 and 9.

To overcome dualism consciously we have to do *exercises of consciousness* that neutralize it at its source by temporarily bridging the chasm that separates the two above-mentioned planes of consciousness. This also solves the riddle of how we as free *individuals* can create something *universal* in our cognition and in the activities based on it. Here, too, the phenomenon of language can serve as a "model" providing new insights. After all, each of us uses language in a highly individual, unique way, and yet language is a phenomenon of community; it is shared by all, and its content is universal.

---

39. Rudolf Steiner, *Goethean Science* (GA 1) (Spring Valley, N.Y.: Mercury Press, 1988), previously translated as *Goethe the Scientist*; *A Theory of Knowledge* (GA 2); *Truth and Knowledge* (GA 3); *The Philosophy of Freedom* (GA 4); *Goethe's World View* (GA 6) (Spring Valley, N.Y.: Mercury Press, 1985).
40. Rudolf Steiner, *A Road to Self-Knowledge* (GA 16) (London: Rudolf Steiner Press, 1975); *The Riddle of Man* (GA 20) (Spring Valley, N.Y.: Mercury Press, 1990); *The Case for Anthroposophy* (GA 21) (London: Rudolf Steiner Press, 1970); *Anthroposophical Leading Thoughts* (GA 26) (London: Rudolf Steiner Press, 1973).

5. The Character of Perceptual Reality

....

To our questioning consciousness the sense-perceptible world appears fraught with questions; how this world becomes questionable was discussed above. In the process, the feeling of reality and the feeling of truth separate; the former remains with the perceptual world while the feeling of truth lights up with our insights and guides them. The sensation of reality also accompanies our perception of man-made objects. We understand these objects in their function. The material they are made of, however, is given in nature or is a modification of something given in nature. Thus, in our perception of these man-made objects a part of them is not permeated with concepts, and this part evokes the feeling of reality in us.

The Sensation of Reality—Observations

It is best to make these observations with *new* perceptions or with the intuitive understanding of *new* ideas, for then we can study the processes in their pure form, without any admixture of other soul processes or habits.

1. The element of the perception that we "understand," the conceptual part, its "what," lies on the same plane of consciousness as all our thoughts. On this plane we also remember

every perception as a representational mental picture. Compared with perceptions, mental pictures do not appear real; they are definitely phenomena of consciousness. Perceptions, however, appear to be really *there*, to be real.

Moreover, we can remember or mentally picture a landscape at any time, but we can see it only in the present moment and when it is present with us. Our mental pictures and our thinking, then, are independent of all external, that is, of all perceptual, factors. Perception, however, does not depend only on us. Therefore the phenomenon of perception has on the one hand the character of the present—in the incomprehensible past—and on the other hand the character of the past—in its conceptuality.

Perception always shows us something "more," and this is precisely what seems to be its nonconceptual part. This may be an illusion, however, because the element which we *experience* is just the aspect which we do not conceive conceptually: namely, the difference between the percept and the mental picture. This incomprehensibility does not necessarily imply that what we do not grasp is actually nonconceptual. To jump to that conclusion has led us from nominalism to materialism, which is convinced that only the *nonideal* or nonconceptual exists and is "real." Instead, we can attribute the incomprehensibility of the percept to the inability of our modern consciousness to grasp living, sentient, and willing—in short, higher—concepts. The concepts we can understand, and also our memory pictures, belong to the plane of the past, and that is why they do not evoke the feeling of reality in us.

2. To experience something as real it must be present in space and time. The temporal present, a point between future and past, is difficult to understand. Spatial presence is also not easy to understand; for instance, we need only ask how far

from us an object can be and still be called "present."[41] This
question, however, reduces the problem to the range of our
senses, and that does not help us, for then we can only say that
we perceive what we perceive.

And yet we apply these incomprehensible concepts "correctly" and understand them when they are used (as, for example, with conjunctions); this points us to the superconscious
sphere, the source of all human capacities and abilities, which
we touched upon in our discussion of concepts (see chapter 2,
"Regarding Concepts"). This superconscious source is the
spiritual part of our soul. We have called the lowest level of
this part that of the present; it is identical with the plane of
imagination.

We can experience the existence and reality of *this* presence
in many phenomena. To express a new thought in time and
space, that is, in speech or writing, we must first have the
thought "beforehand" to be able to find appropriate words and
construct our sentences properly. We are not fully aware of our
thoughts and do not completely understand them until we put
them into words. Nevertheless, we must "conceive" the
thought first before we can express it. The recipients of our
communication then must perform the opposite operation. To
understand the thought we are conveying, they must make
"simultaneous" what appears in time and space as a discontinuous sequence or juxtaposition. Both the sender and the
receiver touch the plane of the present. Although the content
of the communication unfolds time or space in the course of a
sentence, it is nevertheless always "simultaneous," a unity. In
the process of being expressed it is taken apart and brought
into the temporal-spatial world of our senses.

---

41. Massimo Scaligero, *Segreti del Tempo e del Spazio* (Rome: Tilopa, 1964).

In fact, the *content* is as *timeless* as its source. Thus, the essential or eternal present[42] is the source from where the linked duality of time and space—in itself not comprehensible—emerges at the moment when the source is mirrored and no longer experienced as such. After the timeless conception of the meaning of a sentence, the source itself retreats into the superconscious sphere. The fragments of it that appear on the level of the past we call time and space. As we can see in the concept of time, only the past has meaning; the present ("now") and the future respectively can only be imagined as a point and as a continuation of the "time line." Because the past is "past," we no longer have reality in time; the feeling of reality has a source outside of time: in *essential presence*.

Careful observation shows that the spatial dimension is timeless while the dimension of time is outside space. We cannot directly perceive time, that is, movement, process, and change. We perceive only the thing that is being moved, where a process or change is taking place.[43]

This presence is also the source of the feeling of truth or evidence, which is as important in our life as the feeling of reality. It is touched upon in all our statements and stands behind all of them.

---

42. Rudolf Steiner, *The Effects of Spiritual Development* (GA 145) (London: Rudolf Steiner Press, 1978), lecture of March 22, 1913; *Knowledge and Initiation* (GA 211) (Vancouver: Steiner Book Centre, n.d.), lecture of April 14, 1922); *Macrocosm and Microcosm* (GA 119) (London: Rudolf Steiner Press, 1968), lecture of March 30, 1910; *The Michael Mystery* (GA 26) (Spring Valley, N.Y.: St. George Publications, 1984), following leading thoughts 139 and 143; (GA 161, lecture of February 6, 1915); *The Mission of the Archangel Michael* (GA 194) (Spring Valley, N.Y.: Anthroposophic Press, 1961), lecture of November 30, 1919); (GA 214, lecture of August 5, 1922); (G218, lecture of November 17, 1922 and December 9, 1922); *Chance, Providence, and Necessity* (GA 163) (Hudson, N.Y.: Anthroposophic Press, 1988), lecture of August 30, 1915; (GA 183, lecture of August 25, 1918); *Anthroposophy and the Inner Life* (GA 234) (Suffolk, England: Rudolf Steiner Press, 1992), lecture of February 9, 1924.
43. See Kühlewind, *Das Licht des Wortes*, chapters entitled, "Das Leben der Bewusstseinsseele," "Bewegung und Leben," Das Wahrnehmen des Lebens" (Stuttgart: Verlag Freies Geistesleben, 1984).

Thus, the process of perception consists of a past and a present element. The former appears in the conceptuality of the percept and in our options to picture it mentally, both of which participate in the second and all following acts of perception of the same content. The element of the present appears in the feeling of reality that accompanies perception.

3. "Presence" also lights up in thought intuition and understanding. However, because of the flashlike and fleeting character of intuition—its immediate extinction—we do not perceive thoughts as "real." We are conscious only of the results of intuition, on the plane of the past. In our thinking, we strive for intuition, while perception seems more to be given, though it does, of course, require our attention. Thinking attention and perceiving attention differ in that our attention is much more self-conscious in thinking than in perceiving. The reason for this is that our self-awareness is a *thinking* awareness; it awakens in thinking.

There is another difference between thinking and perceiving. The feeling of obviousness or self-evidence that flashes up when we understand is highly differentiated, concrete, and adapted to the manifold possibilities of understanding. In contrast, the sensation of reality in perception is experienced as undifferentiated, or *dull*, precisely because we experience it in not-understanding. This experience is very similar to that of the sense of touch.

4. One can observe that the planes of the past and the present both participate in perception and understanding, although in different ways. Our soul life oscillates in both of these cognitive functions between the two planes. When we understand something through thinking, our soul life briefly touches the superconscious plane of the present and then

remains on the plane of the past until the next act of understanding. When we perceive something, however, this inner
pendulum or oscillation between the planes *continues* for as
long as we are perceiving *attentively*. In perception, we can
experience the phase of surrender to what we perceive more
intensely and not only momentarily—and also experience the
definite return of consciousness to itself. This return coincides
with the conceptual assimilation of what we experienced while
being given over to perception.

These two phases of the activity of consciousness also differ in their degree of wakefulness or self-consciousness. In the
phase of being given over to perception, self-awareness is
asleep; it awakens only in the second phase. Except for special
cases, such as artistic perceptions, or those carried out as a
consciousness exercise, the two phases alternate very quickly
into one another. Still, we can see that the first phase of being
given over to our perception is akin to inhalation—as in aston-
ishment—while understanding, the second phase, is related to
exhalation—as in naming things.[44]

5. While we are given over to what we perceive, we are not
aware of ourselves, and the same is true *during* the act of intuition. Indeed, the more we can "forget" ourselves, the more
intense our act of cognition will be. The result of intuition in
thought is *the understood*, by which consciousness awakens.
The result of perceiving is both the "what" of what we have
perceived—which is conceptual and can originate in our intuitive thinking—and the feeling that the perceived is *real*.

---

44. See Steiner, *A Road to Self-Knowledge* (GA 16), chapter 1; *Study of Man* (GA 293) (London: Rudolf Steiner Press, 1966), lecture of August 29, 1919; *The Philosophy of Freedom* (GA 4), chapters 4 and 6 and Appendix of 1918.

6. Further comparisons reveal that, in thinking, we are dealing only with our own *attention*; it is all that is required for effective thinking. Perception, however, requires the activity of a sense organ in addition to our attention. Usually, people consider only the sense organ, even though it is a fundamental insight for a theory of sensory perception that—as we all notice frequently—even if our sense organs are receptive, we do *not* perceive anything unless our attention is "there" also. Even though all the necessary physical and physiological processes are taking place in the sense organs and in the part of the nervous system connected to them, there is still no perception without attention. These processes may be necessary for perception, but they are not sufficient in themselves to make it happen.

Our thinking is also accompanied by physiological processes in the brain. The source of these processes, however, is not in the external environment; they are activated by thinking itself. As we have discussed in chapter 1, believing that these processes are our thinking or its cause, would lead us merely to an input/output system. This raises the question of the origin of the input; that is, we would have to ask what initiates and controls the physiological processes in the brain. In this brain-based model, "logic" would correspond to physiological lawfulness; in that case, we could neither speak of "logic" nor of physiological laws because both of these require a reference point, a subject, independent of physiology.

7. The two feelings we have discussed, the feeling of evidence and the feeling of reality, cannot be proven, nor can their content; such proof is neither possible nor necessary. Something that is self-evident to us cannot be proven any further beyond that, and we cannot, and do not need to, prove the existence of something our sense of reality tells us is *there*. In

our attempts to develop such proofs, we would only resort again to those two feelings, which we are trying to prove.

The feeling of evidence gives us a degree of certainty in *cognition* that is never achieved in perception. The assertion that "the inductive method never leads to certainty in knowledge" underlies all modern scientific theories. Yet *this* dictum is supposed to be accepted unchallenged as certainty—which shows that in thinking, evidence can indeed lead to definite, certain results, a fact that is often ignored and even denied.

This feeling of evidence applies to what is imperceptible and immaterial. In contrast, the sense of reality seems to apply above all to the material realm. Closer examination, however, shows that what our senses mediate for us—the sensory qualities, the form, or the concept (i.e., the "what" of the percept), and even the feel of the percept in the sense of touch—is also "immaterial."[45]

The feeling of reality originates in the part that is *not* conveyed by the senses, the part we call, rightly or wrongly, the "material." In other words, we do not experience the percept as real because as a "what," as a concept, it lies on the plane of the past: but, we believe the percept exists because we have experienced the sense of reality while we perceived it.

It is easy to see that our higher senses "read" something immaterial out of the "raw material" provided by the lower senses—for example, speech sounds, thoughts, and the identity of (another's) I. We are vaguely aware that the same is true for the middle senses, and this led people to believe that the secondary qualities conveyed by these senses are merely subjective and unreal. Ever since Galileo's time, only those qualities that seemed accessible to the sense of touch were considered as primary, as "real"; of course, this observation is

---

45. See Steiner, *The Riddle of Man* (GA 20), chapter entitled "New Perspectives."

also incorrect. In fact, our sense of touch conveys such undifferentiated impressions that we can say it does not, by itself, really convey anything except the point where our body touches an object. We perceive the object's qualities, such as its roughness, hardness, and so on, only with the help of other senses, such as the sense of movement.

8. Perceptions are often connected with feelings. For the most part, these feelings are "self-feeling," or "self-sensing,"[46] and not cognitive: for example, desires, sympathies, hate, and envy. The other part is "cognitive" and feels the "that" out there, as for example also in passive artistic activity or in the feeling of evidence. In cognitive exercises, too, cognitive feelings are awakened. Both of these feelings—self-feeling and cognitive feeling—are "powerful" because they do not appear on the plane of past consciousness. That is why thoughts are powerless over the self-feeling feelings, which appear as inevitable as percepts. Thoughts can at most hint at what cognitive feelings convey, if they can describe it at all.

In comparison to the two feelings just described, the sense of reality seems to be a third quality. Looking at it with heightened attention, we see that the sense of reality does not appear during the first phase of perception when we are given over to the object of perception. During this phase, we are one with the "object," as we later call it. In this first phase, we are still at one with it *in* reality without noticing it, however. This state is similar to living in a dream reality without realizing it. This phase of perception is a remnant of the soul gesture in the "first" reality.

In the second phase of perception, when we are fully conscious and "within ourselves" and "know" conceptually what

---

46. See Kühlewind, *The Life of the Soul*, chapter 2.

we perceive, we experience reality in contrast to something unreal. The first experience then breaks into, on the one hand, feeling oneself within the body and, on the other, the feeling of reality that applies to objects outside ourselves. Both of these sensations are only vague.

The breaking up of our "first" experience of reality brought about the constellation of touch, namely, the undifferentiated sensation of our own body surface and of the object's surface. Cognizing this, we are led to observe the experience of touch.

9. Of all our senses, the sense of touch is the most self-sensing one; that is, in touching we sense the perceiving organ. We know with which part of our body we are touching something. In contrast, we can observe the function of the eyes or the ears only through experiments guided by our thinking. Accordingly, the sense of touch "tells" us almost nothing about what is perceived except that it is "not me." The sense of touch confronts us with a world outside of ourselves.[47]

What the sense of touch conveys is extreme *otherness*, and therefore it cannot enter our soul immediately. Every other sense communicates a deeper "immersion" into what is being transmitted; the sense of touch, however, makes us aware of the boundary of the body. In the sense of touch, the *balance* between information about what is perceived and self-sensing—which we can easily assess for all our senses—tends toward the extreme of self-sensing. In terms of "egoity" or self-sensing the sense of touch takes first place among the senses. As the intensity of touch increases, the process becomes painful, to the point of being wounding.

Except for the higher senses, which assimilate the material provided by the middle senses, all the other senses can be

---

47. See Steiner, *Anthroposophie: Ein Fragment*, chapter 3.

injured and their normal functioning disrupted by excessive stimulation.[48]

This disruption is almost always due to physical influences. This means that in all sensory activity (excluding the three higher senses), the lower senses, which monitor and regulate the condition of the body—above all, the sense of touch—are to some degree resonating and correspondingly affected. We may not be aware of this cooperation among the senses if the individual organ is not affected more intensely than usual; nevertheless, it is there. Because of this participation of the lower senses, all the other senses also provide self-sensing in addition to the perceptual qualities they convey. The more the lower senses are involved, the less differentiated and expressive will our perception be.

The Functioning of the Human Senses

On the basis of the previous and following observations, we can recognize that the senses are compound formations consisting of a sense organ, whose physical vehicle we can identify more or less exactly,[49] and of our specific, qualitatively differentiated attention, which is instructed in early childhood through higher concepts. That is, children learn *to be attentive* to qualities, for example, to color.

Insofar as the sensory world and its things consist of qualities, particulars ("that") rather than of "substances"—in other words, insofar as they are configurations, "are thus," are

---

48. The sense of movement can be disturbed in connection with other senses, such as the sense of balance. The sense of life can be disrupted through artificially raising or lowering the sensation of life; as a result, its regulative function can cease.

49. Rudolf Steiner, *Die geistigen Hintergründe der Menschlichen Geschichte* (GA 170) (Dornach, Switzerland: Rudolf Steiner Verlag, 1964), lecture of September 2, 1916; and Karl König, *Sinnesentwicklung und Leibeserfahrung* (Stuttgart: Verlag Freies Geistesleben, 1978).

idea-like—we can perceive and know them with the attention of our I-being, which is adapted and qualified to perceive configuration, thusness, and ideas. The sense *organs* by themselves, on the other hand, are not capable of cognizing these, because *ideality can be cognized only by the human spirit, by the I.* Even the elements of things, the sensory qualities, are ideal; therefore our instructed attention is obviously the vehicle for *all* our perceptions. The sense organs, then, have a different function, one that is indispensable for conscious perception. After all, our attention and our sense organs have to work together for conscious perception to come about.

The physical-physiological processes in the sense organs correspond more or less to the physical contact in the sense of touch.

The processes taking place in the brain when we are thinking also correspond to touch. However, these processes are set in motion only by thinking itself. These processes taking place in the brain mirror and, at the same time, immobilize and dull intuitive thinking,[50] which thus sinks down onto the plane of the past. The more intuitive thinking is, the fewer traces it will leave in our physical organism and the more it will free itself from the body.

We do not perceive the physical processes in the brain or those in the sense organs; they are not part of our finished thoughts or our perceptions. Except for higher stages of perception and cognition, we normally become conscious of our finished thoughts only as they are being mirrored. As we have discussed, thoughts themselves cannot originate in the "mirror." Therefore we can discover, in the process of becoming conscious of our thinking, a subtle kind of "touching" that

---

50. See Steiner, *The Riddle of Man* (GA 20), "New Perspectives"; *The Case for Anthroposophy* (GA 21), chapter 1.

evokes self-sensing, albeit much more subtly than physical touching does.

To examine these relations in perception we have to study the two phases of perception separately. Both phases affect the sense organs, and in the second phase the conceptual activity also initiates the processes in the brain that accompany our thinking. These processes do not cause the sensation of reality because it never arises *without* perception. Neither does it originate in the processes in the sense organs; if it did, we would already have the sensation of reality in the first phase of perception, and even in the absence of attention. Therefore, the physiological processes, which cause immobilization and dulling, cannot evoke the sensation of reality. After all, as something *present*, the sensation of reality by definition is not immobilized, dulled, or mirrored—if it were, it would not give us the impression of reality.

The sensation of reality—this may be observed—develops in the second phase of perception, when our soul life is "within ourselves." In this phase, our instructed senses, or our activities of mental representation and association, form concepts and add them to the perceptual world. These concepts developed in modern times are merely substitute concepts, mere names and mental pictures. The plane of the past of our consciousness refuses, filters out, or "dams up" the higher concepts of nature and those of the materials of man-made objects (see chapter 2, "Regarding Concepts"); but it does not immobilize them—in fact, they *cannot* be immobilized precisely *because* they are higher concepts.*

These powerful concepts do not enter the plane of the past. Yet what we have left behind remains alive and retains its character of "presence." It meets the same destiny as that of

---

* See Kühlewind, *The Life of the Soul*, chapter 2. See note 46.

all high inspirations and possibilities we do not seize, even though we could.

The Fate of Higher Ideas

In the past, people did not perceive the same sphere of the world as real that we do. At one time, they experienced the gods as completely real. Much later, universals were considered fundamental realities even though people no longer understood them functionally when they were used as concepts of nature. In those times what appeared to be real but was *conceptless* was called "maya" or illusion. What was then called illusion is identical with what we now take to be solid reality.

Word and world are one in the first phase of the development of consciousness, which has lasting effects that are perceptible in children even in our time. For instance, children, and most adults, easily find their way back into the world of fairy tales, especially if the tales are told with imaginative inner conviction. Every time literature stirs us and evokes our sympathy, it is a faint sign that the magic of the word is working.

The world stage we know later on consists of space and time, the barely graspable fragments of the former unified experience of the world. This is revealed by the fact that we can find neither the *place* nor the *moment* when or where the world becomes a percept. After all, in space and time we can find only temporal-spatial processes that are *already* percepts. We cannot ascertain when and where these processes "change" into processes of consciousness simply because the latter do not originate out of the former but are independent activities.

The great change in our experience of reality occurs gradually, as the abyss between the plane of the present and that of the past forms. The processes of consciousness embed themselves ever more deeply into the physical organism, where they cause increasingly intense physiological processes. As a result, the processes of cognition (attention) are subdued and mirrored:

> In conformity with their original nature, mental pictures [here: ideas] are part of our soul life, but we cannot become conscious of them in the soul unless the soul consciously uses its spiritual organs. So long as the original nature of these mental pictures remains living, the pictures themselves remain unconscious in the soul. The soul *lives* through them but cannot *know* anything of them. To become conscious soul experiences for ordinary consciousness, the pictures must reduce their own life. Such a reduction occurs with every sensory perception. Thus, every time the soul receives a sense impression, the life of the mental pictures is subdued, and the soul consciously experiences this subdued mental picture as the vehicle of a cognition of external reality.[51]

According to spiritual science, we have another relationship to the perceptual world besides the sensory one:

> The intrinsic nature of this [other] relationship does not enter ordinary consciousness. Nevertheless, it exists as a *living*, supersensible connection between us and sensorially perceived objects. What lives in us as a result of this relationship is subdued by our mental organization and turns into a mere "concept." The abstract mental picture is the reality which has died down in order to be represented within ordinary consciousness. Although we live within this reality in sensory perception, we do not become

---

51. See Steiner, *The Case for Anthroposophy* (GA 21), chapter 1.

conscious of it in our lives. An inner necessity of our soul makes our representational mental pictures abstract. Reality gives us something living, and we "deaden" the part of it that falls into our ordinary consciousness.[52]

We can then ask what happens to the part that is not "deadened." When we ascribe real existence to a tree, for example, we do so not on the basis of the relationship between what we see and our eyes. Rather, this judgment about the existence of—in this case—a tree is based on another relationship between ourselves and the object. Ordinary consciousness, however, experiences distinctly and clearly only the first relationship—between our eyes and the tree we see. The other relationship remains dim and subconscious; it manifests only in the *result*, that is, in our acknowledgment of the "green tree" as really existing. In fact, every percept that leads to such a judgment is based on a *twofold relationship* between ourselves and the world of objects.[53]

In the first phase of perception—when we are given over to the object—this twofold relationship consists, on the one hand, in sensing the processes in the sense organs (which we know from physiology) and, on the other hand, in the processes of attention, or the I. The actual perceiving takes place in these attentional processes, and we become conscious of it when it is mirrored by the ones in the sense organs. In the second phase of perception, the processes in our brain accompanying our conceptual activity reduce or dim part of the attentional processes. The concepts formed there are of a past character, and we have therefore called them substitute concepts.

The part of the perceptual process that is not dimmed and reduced consists of the powerful ideas standing behind the

---

52. Ibid., chapter 4.3.
53. Ibid., chapter 4, and see also *Anthroposophie: Ein Fragment*, Appendix.

phenomena of nature. These ideas are analogous to the functional ideas behind man-made objects. They are not "grasped" or "conceived," yet enter our consciousness through the senses—not through the sense *organs*—albeit only in metamorphosed form. To gain a clearer understanding of this metamorphosis, we will briefly discuss the nature of these ideas.

When we conceive a new idea, a "clear and bright" will is doubtlessly active in this production. The cognitive feeling of evidence guides the intuition in our thinking. In other words, the three soul functions of thinking, feeling, and willing form a unity in the act of intuition, but they break apart in our mirrored consciousness. Similarly, we can expect—and observation confirms this—that the ideas behind nature address all three human soul functions. A firm, unchanging creational will stands behind every natural phenomenon,[54] and we adapt our will to this will of the world. "In experiencing the process [of the perception of nature], we realize that through this reversal of our will, our soul takes hold of a spiritual element outside itself."[55]

The feeling of the cosmic word, the phenomena of nature, develops into the undifferentiated but living sense of reality—whose development we shall consider later. Thoughts that are not understood become "images" of nature, for example, "audible" or "smell" images, and so on—written or spoken signs we do not understand and cannot "read-together" or integrate and that we try to guess at with our substitute concepts.

As we have seen, the more intensely our senses are affected, the more their functioning tends to be disturbed and exposed to pain and injury. Now we will examine what happens when we

---

54. See Steiner, *The World of the Senses and the World of the Spirit* (GA 134) (Spring Valley, N.Y.: Anthroposophic Press, 1979), lecture of December 28, 1911; *The Mission of the Archangel Michael* (GA 194), lecture of November 30, 1919; *Study of Man* (GA 293), lecture of August 23, 1919.
55. See Steiner, *The Riddle of Man* (GA 20), "New Perspectives."

enhance the quality on the other branch of the twofold relationship, namely, in the activity of our attention.

Ancient science investigated the hierarchy of the senses starting from the lower senses and proceeding upward. It examined their "why," their intention, but ultimately their investigation was aimed at the "who" of this intention. The impressions transmitted by the middle senses were considered a system of *signs that one could read.* Cognition was the investigation of this speech or writing of the gods—of its meaning. Cognition dealt with ideas. During that period people knew from experience that ideas do not emerge accidentally, independently of a person. Therefore, they spoke of the I-related idea, the *word.* The world was wordlike, word-natured. Cognition, then, was a dialogue with nature; people sensed creative beings—or at least their representatives: nature beings, such as nature gods, mountain gods, river gods or spirits—behind nature.

However, the above-mentioned transformation of our consciousness caused the language concepts concerning nature to dry up into mere names. As a result, the former perceptual world of signs turns into one of *things.* And as this happens, the dialogue with nature ends because if the perceptual world consists of things rather than ideas, then no beings stand behind our percepts. Our investigation no longer proceeds in an upward movement. What was formerly considered raw material provided by the middle senses or the sense of touch now itself becomes "the reality." It is no longer complemented with ideas—or so it seems.

In truth, however, we simply fail to notice that this "reality" is interwoven with ideas. Nevertheless, this "reality" is endowed with the feeling of reality, which originates in the higher, comprehending, yet dreamlike participation in the perceptual world, an experience not accompanied by self-awareness and still part of a unified existence. The higher feeling of evidence developed into the sensation of reality accompanying our percepts. At the same time, our increasing capacity to be aware of our body grew into the above-described self-sensing (see also chapter 7).

Today, the twelve senses define twelve separate realms of experience in the adult; there are almost no transitions between these realms. In contrast, the sensory system of children—and of people in ancient times—is organized differently; they are basically all sense organ.* In children and in ancient peoples, the twelve senses are not yet separated. Moreover, there were other qualities in addition to the twelve senses that have later disappeared, namely, the transitions between those senses. The senses that later became the upper senses, such as the sense for the I (of another being) or the sense for concepts, are active *within* the middle and the lower ones. As a result, perception is filled with ideas and pertains to beings. Of course, it is not "filled with ideas" in our modern sense of the phrase; rather, we find an echo of this condition in artistic activity.

Even though the senses separate later, they still work together, each conveying "raw material" upward, to the next higher senses and ultimately to the I-sense. This explains the characteristic questions of ancient science. With the further development of consciousness, however, the senses cease to work together, and each now remains, to begin with, without any definite direction at all.

Thereafter, an impulse we do not have to describe in more detail here[56] leads to a tendency to explain everything from below, by mechanical effects. This tendency typically asks

---

* See note 22.

56. See Steiner, *Three Streams in Human Evolution* (GA 184) (London: Rudolf Steiner Press, 1965), lectures of October 11 and 12, 1918; *The Michael Mystery* (GA 26), following leading thought 173 [March 29, 1925]; *How Do I Find the Christ* (GA 182) (New York: Anthroposophic Press, 1941), lecture of October 16, 1918; (GA 211, lecture of June 11,1922).

"what is it made of?" or "what causes it?" This turning of our gaze toward *things* reveals a will hostile to the word. Analogously, the thinking or perceiving person has the inclination to reduce human spiritual capacities and achievements to physical and physiological causes. Higher ideas (and ideality as such) are rejected, though they continue nevertheless to be an *active*, powerful force. Now, however, they are compelled to exert their metamorphosed influence in the depths of the *subconscious* part of the soul. We can see this in the feeling of reality, which is inseparably connected with the act of perception.

Regarding the senses, it may be said that, since the higher ideas are not "understood" or taken in by the higher senses, they turn to the middle and lower senses, leaving an "impression" upon them. As this "pressure" is passed down through the ladder of the senses, it becomes more and more material and increasingly resembles the impression of physical touch.[57] When this "pressure" reaches the lower senses, particularly the sense of touch, the typical sensation of reality appears.

Still, the lower senses participate weakly in every sense perception;[58] in fact, all the senses are always to some extent involved in perception although one sense definitely predominates. For example, when we do not understand our partner in a conversation, we hear only words, his or her voice. In other words, the percept begins to descend the ladder of the senses. In the same way, people who cannot read see only the black shapes of the letters on the page.

The power of the ideas of nature not only gives us the sense of reality, but it also enables us to perceive in the first place. These willing, sensing, and living ideas create forms of will, sensation, and life—that is, the mineral, animal, and plant kingdoms—and are active within them. Our attention can

---

57. See Steiner, *Anthroposophie: Ein Fragment* (GA 45), chapter 6.
58. See Steiner, *The Case for Anthroposophy* (GA 21), chapter 4.

unite itself with these ideas; however, we are usually conscious only of that part of an encounter that has been subdued
by its physical and physiological effects. Nowadays, our
senses function only when they are affected by the mineral-
physical influence of nature and in this way assist our attention. Thus, we can describe the share of attention in perception
as follows: "Perception is the boundary where our thoughts
touch the creative thoughts outside."[59]

Our ordinary thinking, which belongs to the plane of the
past, takes us to the boundary of the perceptible, which is alive
and therefore cannot be comprehended by our thinking. Perception, then, begins at the point beyond which thinking cannot penetrate into the creative—arrested—cosmic thinking.

Thus, we can think of perception as a continuous intuition,
for which the senses keep the entrance open. The part of perception that is not understood becomes what is perceptible;
it *is* perceptibility itself. In other words, we approach the
perceptual world like a meditative sentence we read only
for its informational content. Its higher meaning thus remains
hidden because it does not emerge unless the activity of our
consciousness complements the perceptible part of the sentence on the appropriate level.

In the process of perception, this higher meaning appears
as a picture that is incomprehensible for ordinary thinking—
it appears as percept. Because it is not understood, this picture
is interwoven with high concepts; after all, it consists of sensory qualities. However, these concepts permeating the picture
are unthinkable for the plane of the past of our consciousness.
They do not suffice to understand the meaning of phenomena

---

59. Rudolf Steiner, *Foundations of Esotericism* (GA 93a) (London: Rudolf Steiner
Press, 1982), lecture of October 12, 1905; and *Spiritual Science as a Foundation for
Social Forms* (GA 199) (Hudson, N.Y.: Anthroposophic Press, 1986), lectures of
August 8 and 14, 1920.

of nature. We can attempt to let this meaning take hold of us through perceptual meditation or pure perception.[60]

The further down we move along the scale of the senses, the poorer the sensory field will be in named concepts. For example, in German we have seven colors for the sense of sight, three or four words to describe the impressions of the sense of taste, but not even one for the sense of smell. The reason is that the latter senses are addressed by very high ideas that do not enter our mirrored consciousness. Conscious spiritual development will give these senses particular significance.[61]

The concepts belonging to the senses are increasingly powerful the lower we descend in the hierarchy of the senses. Higher meaning participates faintly, and usually unnoticed, in every act of human perception.

Understandably, then, the sense of touch, which conveys the smallest amount of information about the percept to our ordinary consciousness, radiates a sense of being filled with the *feeling for God* into our soul—"the feeling of being filled with being as such."[62]

It is the metamorphosis of the creational ideas that causes the ordinary sensation of touch while the unmetamorphosed quality resonates faintly in the upper realm of the soul. This is true for all the senses: what they convey to consciousness is always accompanied—as though by an overtone—by a higher, at first incomprehensible, quality.

60. Rudolf Steiner, *The Boundaries of Natural Science* (GA 322) (Hudson, N.Y.: Anthroposophic Press, 1983), lectures of October 2 and 3, 1920. See also this book, chapter 10.
61. Rudolf Steiner, *The Riddle of Humanity* (GA 170) (London: Rudolf Steiner Press, 1990), lecture of August 13, 1916.
62. See Steiner, *Spiritual Science as a Foundation for Social Forms*, lecture of August 8, 1920.

The Wordlike Character of Nature

Wherever we find qualities, similarity, differences, question-ableness, analogy, homology, relationship, we also find ideas. To our questions concerning nature we do not expect a "some-thing" but a conceptual answer, just as our question was also a conceptual one. Wherever we find ideas, the Word or word-will of I-beings is or was active. In the "first reality," language assured the wordlike character of the world by structuring and integrating the given world as a whole, of which language itself is a part. Therefore world and language must match or harmonize. The one original language, however, has branched out into a variety of languages, and all of them are suited to their own world as well as to that of other languages. None of these languages is lacking anything.

Accordingly, the basic structure of nature corresponds to the common element that stands behind all languages. This com-mon element does not necessarily appear in the sense-percepti-ble part of languages; it lies in their totality, which comprises both the hidden and the perceptible parts. Nature and lan-guages have a common source; this is the message of the first verses of the prologue of the Gospel of St. John. By implica-tion, then, the language of nature is not identical with any of the languages we human beings speak. To understand the lan-guage of nature requires raising cognition above and beyond these languages.

6. The Development of I-Consciousness

....

Perception and thinking exist only for *someone* to the extent that they manifest in a human, i.e., discontinuous form. They adopt such a form by being "wordlike." "Wordlike" here does not, of course, refer to the appearing part of a word but to the pattern-configuration or ideal character of every form of language, whose appearance consists of words, sounds, sentences, structures, discontinuities, and connections. From this we can already see that human attention is an attention for what is word-natured. Indeed, transparent consciousness contains only what is wordlike, "wording" elements, even though there is not necessarily a corresponding word for each of these elements in our languages.

The attention that is open to what is wordlike is a faculty of the I; we could also call it the primal substance of the I. But this "substance"—what is attention made *of*?—develops into an I only if it becomes conscious self-experience. For this our attention to the "other," [the external object], must be interrupted. For if the attention is continuously given over to the "other," there can be no self-experience. Here, too, discontinuity is necessary.

This kind of discontinuity, however, does not simply develop as a result of learning to speak and so does not arise from the mastery of the organs of speech and movement. Although our sense of movement is essential for the purposeful movements of the speech and other organs, this in itself does not yet lead to conscious self-experience. Through the sense of movement we "perceive," and thus control, our organism's own movements; this enables us to carry out specific movements without having to call on any other senses, such as the sense of sight.

Attention that is open and receptive must be interrupted. The inflow of the given—of all wordlike entities—into the inner and outer senses must cease and start up again in rhythmic intervals. Sleep creates such a stop in our attention's dedication. When we are asleep, our attention withdraws from the senses to its original sphere, the realm of the superconscious. Thus, during sleep we do not experience attention consciously, but only superconsciously. When we awaken it returns, gradually bringing more and more superconscious content with it. Eventually, our waking attention cannot help noticing that it has been interrupted.

At first the discontinuity seems to be only a gap. Within this gap our attention then creates an "object" out of itself. It is the change in awareness, in fact, that makes our attention an "object" for itself. We are then able to "notice" independently, and without any "given," the part of our attention that works in the superconscious realm even when we are awake. This superconscious part of our attention structures the perceptual given and "reads it together" or synthesizes it, and it is this inner act, the reading itself, of which we then become conscious.

At the beginning of the development of consciousness—in childhood and in ancient humanity—we notice this inner act only fleetingly and only at the periphery of our consciousness. The awareness is clothed in divine, then in semidivine, form; we sense it only faintly in cognitive feelings, initially as a gap among the given sensations, as our separate self.

As this awareness of the gap becomes independent of outer conditions, it becomes an inner experience. In the course of the development of our consciousness, this inner experience—

which became inner experience because it began to be independent from the given elements—changes into the duality of mind (intellect) and soul (or heart). At first, the soul is still experienced as a perceptive cloud of feeling that inspires the intellect. However, in the age of the *consciousness soul* the living, unreflecting mind subdivides into two planes of consciousness, that of the past—with its clear outlines, on which we moderns mostly "live" and of which we are conscious— and that of the present, which we can also call the imaginative plane, which has nowadays shifted into the superconscious realm. Every understanding and every intuition comes from this plane of the present like a flash of grace. This plane is also the source of the superconscious "how" of our thinking, and every intuition, every new idea, is actually a condensation of this "how."

Along with the separation of mind into past and present, the soul or heart—not today's soul, but the cognizing soul—also subdivides: into cognitive feeling and self-sensing feeling. Cognitive feeling lives above the plane of the present; self-sensing feeling belongs to the plane of the past and is part of the subconscious of the modern soul. Therefore it is aware of *itself*—rather than of *something out there*—in emotions such as envy, ambition, and so on.

Since the plane of the present has now moved into the superconscious realm, a change from one plane to the other makes discontinuities possible, even when we are fully awake and conscious. To remain conscious, our consciousness must at least briefly touch the level of the present repeatedly. If it remained continually on the level of the past, our consciousness would no longer be "conscious." This is how the structure and capacity typical of the consciousness soul develop: namely its ability to reflect upon itself, to look from the plane of the present onto that of the past, and to experience—at the periphery of consciousness—the plane of the present in touch with the plane of the past.

The ability to reflect on thinking, language, and consciousness has led to the development of the sciences typical of the age of the consciousness soul—e.g., epistemology, linguistics, and psychology. The I becomes a reality through this ability of conscious reflection; it realizes itself when the given part of the I, that is, attention, is actually connected with the idea of the I. This is analogous to how we realize a word or a text; we connect the perceptible part of the word or text—the given—with the meaning from which it has been separated in the act of being expressed.

The *real* connection of attention to the idea of the I can occur only on the plane of the present, in the experience of living thinking, perceiving, or mental representation. After all, as we saw above, the term "reality" does not apply to the plane of the past. The idea of the true I lights up only in these experiences on the plane of the present. However, it is preceded by preliminary I-experiences that are reflected in the various definitions of the I in the course of the development of consciousness.

The idea of each I-being, which becomes connected with the given of the I, the attention, is entirely individual. I-beings are not a species. As I-beings, each of us belongs to his or her own species, which consists of only one specimen. This fact is reflected in the individuality of our names; unlike all other nouns, our names are the only concepts, the only words, that do not have a general meaning.

7. Self-Sensing

The I's experience of itself creates the I; for without knowing of itself, an I-being cannot be a reality. Nevertheless, self-experience is hardly ever realized in its pure form, not even in its preliminary stages. This is because another, parallel process occurs as we take hold of the body through the I when we learn to speak. This other process has no direct connection to speaking and is thus not caused by it. Rather, this second process grows from the temptation of the I to sense itself in the body it has taken hold of and to enjoy this sensation.

To move the limbs purposefully, the I-being must control and direct them. This it does through the sense of movement. The senses are the cognitive functions of sensation; they provide cognitions without current intellectual activity. For this purpose they have free (cognitive) powers of sensitivity that are not engaged in controlling biological functions. In these powers the I can express and articulate itself.

As far as movements are concerned, we human beings can imitate all forms of movement. The sense of our own movements acts through powers of sensation that "sense" the movements of our organs and can thus control or direct them. This "sensing" does not become the above-mentioned self-sensing because, paradoxically, we do not feel it as a sensation. For instance, when we write or play the violin, we are not usually aware of our hands; our movements are controlled superconsciously.

These superconscious powers of sensation, which are not focused on themselves, become self-sensing when the I-being *mixes* with them and with the powers of sensation of its biological being—which in themselves are not self-sensing either—rather than simply directing them and learning from them about the body's movements. In the process, these cognitive forces, which are usually directed outward, develop an "irregular" center, group themselves around it, and lose their original outer-directed focus. That is, they turn into egotistical self-sensing. In contrast to the I, the resulting formation can be called the "ego"; it is an attention focused on itself, one that is not cognitive but merely self-sensing.

This self-sensing develops without our conscious intention, and we remain unconscious of its consequences. After all, nobody *wants* to be envious, vengeful, or power-hungry. In contrast to our superconscious capacities or powers, this whole sphere is called the subconscious. It consists of *formed* sensations, inclinations, and instinctive, compelling sensation "intentions" that urge us to repeat them. Since all of these are already fully formed, they are not cognitive.

The development of the subconscious follows as a result of this self-sensing. In the subconscious realm, free cognitive forces, of which the I has not consciously taken hold, mass together out of egoity. Modern human beings must do something with these forces by themselves. In earlier times, they were still controlled and ordered through the superconscious. In the animal kingdom we find virtually no instincts or passions that are harmful to the animals' health or biological organism. Such instincts and passions can exist only when forces usually serving the biological organism become free and undefined through the presence of the I, but are not used by the I.

In children these forces still function as undivided forces of attention. This is the reason why children can learn to speak and to think with such unparalleled ease. This is also the reason why adults no longer have this wonderful ability. In part, indeed for the most part, the above-mentioned forces are transformed, in adults, into self-sensing ones, and the attention is split and divided between world and egoity.

Self-sensing is possible only for I-beings. The sensations of animals are completely preformed and serve only their biological life. Animals have no freedom in sensation—they can only react. Thus, they cannot distinguish between sensation caused by inner sources and those caused by outer sources. Always, their whole sensitivity reacts and is active. There is no uninvolved, free entity that could be aware of or experience such reactions. Therefore, we find egoity only in I-beings. The ego is the reflected, self-sensing form of the I; it is self-sensing instead of self-aware.[63]

---

63. Self-sensing and self-awareness, or ego-consciousness and I-consciousness, are described in detail in *The Philosophy of Freedom* (GA 4), chapter 5.

8. Changes in the Given

The planes of the past and the present, which are separated in the consciousness soul,[64] were still intermingled or mixed in the mind-soul. The process of thinking was then still *given* to human beings. Today thinking enters consciousness *superconsciously* from the plane of the present—that is, without our awareness. Formerly, because of the mixed structure of the mind-soul, the process of thinking was given to people in a dreamlike manner, without clear outlines, and people could not hold their own in this process. Their experience resembled the way we experience ourselves when we dream. Words and concepts were one. They were experienced as they *arose*, as they entered consciousness. Nowadays, we understand words and concepts in the same way too, but for us their entry into consciousness remains superconscious. We are clearly conscious only of their result, of what we *have understood*; of course, by then this has lost its life and become dead. Because of children's dreamlike experience of these processes, their soul life is alive in a way that adults have lost.

Similarly, before the soul separated into cognitive and self-sensing feelings, the experience of evidence in the field of religion was given to people in the form of "faith." Our experience of evidence in mathematics or logic is a vestige of this.

---

64. See Kühlewind, *Das Licht des Wortes,* chapter entitled "Das Leben der Bewusstseinsseele."

Once cognitive feeling has moved into the superconscious realm, divinity is no longer *given*. In earlier periods of the development of consciousness, divinity was given, as we can see, for example, in the continuous intervention of the Homeric gods in human destiny and in the speaking of the godhead to people in the Old Testament. Nowadays, we become conscious of what enters our consciousness from the superconscious realm only on the plane of the past. This makes it impossible for us to experience the cognitive processes of consciousness, or to experience life or being.

At the same time, another change has taken place in the configuration of the soul, namely, the general development of the subconscious in the last two hundred years or so. This conglomeration of habits extends from the domain of associations through self-sensing feelings and complexes to a deep layer that can be called "collective," at least as far as our culture is concerned. This layer is the foundation of all other subconscious formations, but it is not the same as Jung's "collective unconscious." Since this layer is truly collective, we can perceive it only under special conditions, for example, through enhanced attention that remains awake without being mirrored.

The more individual layers of the subconscious send their impulses into consciousness by means of the self-sensing feelings and the will at their disposal. The collective subconscious, on the other hand, manifests itself above all in thought formations that are generally accepted as plausible and convincing based on collective sensations; in fact, however, these thought formations are at least as irrational as the more individual impulses of the subconscious. We cannot reason out these thought formations consequentially; their persuasive power is not connected to the feeling of evidence that guides logical or intuitive thinking.

Thus, what is given to us from above, from the supercon-scious, is joined by what is "given" from below, from the subconscious. Indeed, what is given from the subconscious now plays a leading role in human life and has become a world power. Human beings now live by secondary instincts and passions, originating in the subconscious. Our thinking could help us orient ourselves, but it has been influenced by what comes out of the subconscious and now accepts and spreads so-called insights and new dogmas as knowledge. As a result, the inclinations, habits, and addictions originating in our sub-conscious gain scientific justification.

We do not learn to speak and think "by nature" but by edu-cation and the imitation of models. Similarly, everything in human development, the good and the bad, comes about through education. For example, certain individuals, our fore-runners in the history of thought—inspired by powers unknown to them—developed trains of thought that then elab-orated and coached our collective subconscious impulses.

All inspirations and thoughts that are prompted by our col-lective subconscious share two characteristic features: they cannot be thought through logically—that is, thinking can penetrate them only up to a certain limit—and they give the *sensation* of an overwhelming persuasive power that covers up the fact that we cannot really think them through. We have good reason to assume a subconscious origin for every impenetrable, incomprehensible thought, or train of thought. The whole sphere of egoity is connected to the subconscious. People do not decide to become egoists; it happens without our will.

This twofold change in the given—the shift of both the *pro-cess* of thinking and cognitive feeling into the superconscious and the arising of the subconscious—admonishes us to change our attitude and behavior toward it. Only a free being, or one that is at least partially free, can "change" anything. We have this potential because of the dual-track structure of the consciousness soul. We are protected from direct spiritual impulses because their source has shifted into the superconscious realm, and we can protect ourselves from subconscious impulses by being *moral* in our thinking and cognition, that is, by "conscientiously" examining and testing whether something can be thought through to the end, and accepting it as a thought only if this is indeed the case.

We begin to realize for the first time that we have the possibility to educate ourselves when we experience our *freedom in cognition*. After all, cognition must be free; otherwise we could not determine whether it is truth or error, and we could not evaluate its results. If all human cognition, including thinking itself, consisted of natural processes, we could not speak of knowledge at all because natural as well as mechanical processes just run their course; they cannot err, they are simply conditioned. Moreover, we could not possibly evaluate the "knowledge" resulting from natural processes because the evaluation would have to be based on other, but equally conditioned, natural processes. Speaking, in the human sense, would also be impossible, and even the silence, which could result from such a so-called insight, would be contradictory precisely because of this insight. In other words, we could not take any logical stance since we would be denying our ability to draw logical and consistent conclusions.

Thinking cannot deny or even limit thinking, just as a word cannot rob itself of its meaning. And thinking could only be dethroned by thinking; the word could only be dethroned by the word.

This fundamental insight leads us toward the *sources of thinking*. From this insight it is clear that thinking cannot *prove* itself, and the same insight shows the impossibility to deny the independence and irreducibility of thinking. At this point, we have to decide to begin our self-education precisely with the education of our capacity for cognition, a decision that implies the continuation of the activity we have recognized so far as our only free one.

To approach the superconscious process of thinking more closely, we have to raise our *level* of consciousness. The first question is whether it is possible to do so. This question must be answered in the affirmative *before* we take this step—if the step is to be taken legitimately—that is, if it is to be thought through to the end conscientiously and so made secure.

The "how" of our thinking is given (see chapter 2), and we use this "how"—the logic of thinking—as a superconscious ability to think based on evidence and logicalness without, however, being able to explain or account for it. Thus, the "how" of thinking is one of the "signs of transcendence" that we can find *empirically* in ourselves.[65] Indeed, it is the most fundamental of these signs, and we can find and understand all the other signs with the help of this one.

In more than one sense, our thinking is *discontinuous*. To clarify our thinking for ourselves or for others, we have to articulate it in thoughts and express it through compound sentences, sentences, and words, all of which consist of parts and are thus discontinuous. *Before* we express something, however, we must have the meaning to be expressed; otherwise we could not put it into words or formulate it. For example, we could not ascertain whether our formulation is correct or, as sometimes happens, inadequate. To make such an evaluation, we have to compare the discontinuous expression to something we are not yet fully conscious of, something that is not yet a finished thought and is therefore not on the plane of the

65. See P. L. Berger, *A Rumor of Angels*, (New York: Bantam, Doubleday, Dell, 1981).

past. This "something" consequently does not have a discontinuous form; nevertheless, it must exist superconsciously, at the periphery of our consciousness. In a good translation it is this "meaning" that is transferred into another language.

Meaning, unlike its expression (in one or more sentences), is a *continuum*. However, it is not totally unstructured; after all, its latent structure unfolds in the discontinuity of language. The continuum is primary while the expression is secondary. As we understand a text we read or hear, this continuum is reproduced in us.

Conceiving—intuiting—a meaning, expressing it in a discontinuous form, as well as reading a text and reproducing its meaning, all require *attention*. The meaning that we conceive is *wordlike*; that is, it *says* something. If it were not so, the meaning could not result in the expression—there would be nothing there that could be said in the words of a language. In this way "greater" or "mightier" words descend from the superconscious into consciousness, that is, into discontinuous form. Our understanding of a text, on the other hand, ascends from its discontinuous expression to the more continuous meaning. In this "ascent," consciousness moves from word to word, without leaving or forgetting the preceding words, but also without "remembering" them. The movement of understanding proceeds superconsciously, outside of time; it does not follow the temporal sequence of the sense-perceptible words[66] but retains and anticipates them in a timeless present. The expression of the intuition flows from this timeless present into temporality. Thus, our attention alternates between continuity and discontinuity.

Our attention alternates in another way also because every element of discontinuity—be it thoughts, the perceptual world,

---

66. See Kühlewind, *Das Licht des Wortes,* chapter "Bewegung und Leben."

or a text—offers an opportunity for our attention to become distracted from our consciously chosen subject. We can direct our attention to anything we choose; however, as we know from experience, it is difficult to keep our attention focused on an uninteresting and unappealing theme. Associations influencing us from the subconscious realm of the soul distract us against our conscious will and our conscious intention.

The discontinuous form of attention in thinking, representing, and perceiving makes it possible for these activities to proceed *step by step* in understanding, thereby freeing these functions from the necessity of understanding immediately and intuitively. At the same time, this discontinuous form offers our subconscious impulses the opportunity to intervene in the flow of the attention we have consciously directed in a particular way. This in turn restricts the autonomy of our consciousness in controlling and maintaining our attention.

At first, attention cannot experience and meet itself in its discontinuous form; it cannot meet itself (see chapter 6) because it is constantly interrupted. Our attention is continuously falling out of its present and leaves its traces as a past—for example, in finished thoughts, percepts, mental representations. This development was necessary for the sake of the growth of I-consciousness.

Once we have learned discontinuous, conceptual thinking and have become able to synthesize, and once this has brought us to the structure of the consciousness soul, we can continue the further development of consciousness through conscious schooling. For, by this time, because of the structure of the consciousness soul, we no longer receive anything positive from the given *without effort on our part*. Our first goal has to be to strengthen the autonomy of our consciousness, that is, to strengthen our attention, a considerable part of which is caught in subconscious formations and habits.

We can realize this goal by concentrating our attention on objects that are not appealing or interesting in themselves. For this, we must choose things that we can completely think through. Man-made objects with their functional ideas are appropriate for such exercises.[67]

To avoid becoming distracted we must picture the object and think thoughts proper and relevant to it as a *preparatory* exercise. The actual concentration on the function or idea of the object, however, requires that our now-strengthened attention become more continuous. We cannot "think" an idea, such as an invention, or the function of an object, with interruptions because it is neither a word nor a picture. That is also why the idea or function cannot be remembered or repeated; rather, it requires continuous intuition.

To ensure that an idea *stays* in our consciousness, our concentrated attention must *stay* in the immediate present. The mental image and thought of the object, as well as its idea, are woven out of our attention; they *are* this attention. That is why we must make our attention more and more continuous through these exercises. Then, with the help of the idea as subject to focus on, we raise our attention to the continuity of the immediate present.

Our consciousness thus arrives at the "how" of thinking, which is the logic of the discontinuous expression of our thoughts. The functional idea of the man-made object is given to us superconsciously in childhood as our ability-to-cognize all similar objects as the same. Now we seek to raise our consciousness to a level that is usually superconscious.

This answers the question of whether thinking consciousness can come closer to its sources. It also allows us to

---

67. See Kühlewind, *Stages of Consciousness*, chapter entitled "Concentration and Contemplation."

describe the self-awareness of the I, which was mentioned in chapter 5, in more detail. When we practice the exercises presented above, we realize that the theme we pictured or thought of, especially the idea of the chosen object, consists of attention. This attention is concentrated by virtue of the theme and simultaneously focused on it. In other words, our attention is focused on itself. We can now experience and perceive it just like any other percept, because it has been strengthened within itself. In our attention's encounter with itself, the idea of the I lights up and is realized. This is how our experience of the I on the level of the immediate present develops.

This experience is fundamental to our pursuit of spiritual science.[68]

Nevertheless, another experience precedes it, namely, the insight that our thinking and representing attention is a more powerful reality than the thought or pictured theme because the latter is brought forth or maintained by this attention.

While attention cannot experience its own discontinuity because it is continuously falling out of the reality of the timeless present into the unreality of the past, it can nevertheless develop toward continuity by exercising. The less attention is interrupted—the less discontinuous it is—the more alive and present it becomes and the closer it moves toward the experience of evidence and of itself. Evidence is the property of reality; in other words, reality is self-evident. This points to the one and common source for reality—its effective cause—and the cognition of it. Reality actuates the cognition of itself. But in the process of cognition, "reality" *becomes* reality (see chapter 4). Cognizing and cognized reality coincide and become one; they are one in our experience of them in the immediate present: they *are* this experience.

---

68. Ibid., chapter entitled "The Fundamental Experience of the Spirit."

We can also say that in cognizing we realize ourselves in living self-cognition; this is the source of evidence. In cognizing we become one with what we cognize, or cognizing cognizes *itself* rather than something else, because it itself *becomes* the "otherness" that is cognized and that ceases to be "other" in the process of cognition. The feeling of evidence originates in this realized and experienced identity.

On the level of the pure sciences, such as mathematics, logic, and geometry, it is clear that the objects of cognition are created by our cognition itself; and their "cognition" is at the same time their creation, which occurs intuitively—through thought or representational intuition. Afterward, "reasoning" can build the steps to bridge the great leap of intuition. This experience in the sciences corresponds to the realization that the objects on which we focus our thinking and representing attention consist of this same attention.

On higher planes of knowledge, the unity of cognition and its "object" is experienced more and more intensely, up to the experience of evidence. Thinking and perception also approach each other, and coincide in the intuition; in our ordinary cognition subject and object appear separated because thinking and perception are separated. As a result of the intuition, the experience of evidence in the central point of the I falls, like a shadow, into the plane of the past, and is there experienced without its reality-of-being; but at least we *experience* it. Whenever something like this experience occurs, the shadow of self-evidence may be felt.

Proofs and the necessity to prove things are phenomena of modern consciousness. Intuition and genius are higher and more continuous forms of attention. They evolve their theses, for example, those of mathematics, in *one* great step. Proofs, on the other hand, are for those who cannot take the big step—the big insight—all at once, in one leap. These steps form discontinuities, and every one of these interruptions in the process of understanding—every step along the way—offers new opportunities for error; one does not immediately understand the whole proposition, but one can comprehend the evidence of the individual steps. Since we do not understand the thesis as a whole, even one unnoticed wrong step in the proof can be enough to "prove" a wrong thesis. Our attention rests at every connecting link between the steps in the proof. These connecting points easily allow incorrect turns, or "ideas" that have not been thoroughly tested and thought through, to enter in. Upon closer examination, such turns and "ideas" reveal themselves as unthinkable—or would be unthinkable if we examined them—and they disrupt our train of thought with prejudices, emotional bias, or wishful thinking. After all, the steps of the proof must be connected logically. Since these connections are usually not explicit, they are rarely examined and we are content with a kind of "common sense," or with appeals to habitual forms of thinking.

As we saw in chapter 3, language structures our perceptual world. However, the *meaning* of the designating words may have changed in the course of the evolution of human consciousness—even though they may have retained their outer form, and their sense may seem unchanged. *This* kind of change is not even suspected by linguists because they are stuck in our modern consciousness. The change I am referring to here is the change in our relationship to these word-concepts as well as to the natural phenomena they designate.

For us, the names of objects in nature indicate *things*. For instance, the word "oak" now refers to a particular individual tree, and when we use the word to talk about the *genus* oak, it seems to us an abstraction. For ancient humanity the reverse was the case. Then, the word "oak" was primarily a real universal, an idea manifested in the phenomenal world in many specimens. That is, "oak" then was not a "name" (as it now is for us) but a character, a function, a meaningful designation of a relationship and connection. For us the "oak" remains external; we find it "thinkable" not in itself but only on account of its outer characteristics. In fact, we think of the oak—in contrast to the ideas and functions of man-made objects or mathematical concepts—only nominalistically.

Formerly, natural phenomena were seen and understood not as things but primarily as relations. That is, they were understood more as a continuity. Nowadays, however, we perceive particulars, individual things, as the primary given. Then we try to find the connections between them in the sphere of mechanics, rather than *reading* them on the model of language, of linguistic and textual interconnections, as people in ancient times did. If we do not read a text, it stands out as something existential. Only through our reading does a text become truth. The perceptual world of nature is difficult to read because of its initially discontinuous structure, which is largely a result of inadequate concepts.

9. Meditation

....

The more discontinuous thinking becomes, the more it moves away from the experience of evidence. This explains why recent philosophy can deny the existence of evidence in its thinking—even though this thinking, in its activity, continuously resorts to its own intrinsic evidence. The gaps in our attention allow such nonthoughts—which resemble thoughts only in their form—to creep into our consciousness. At the same time, these "pauses" in our dedication also offer our attention the opportunity to notice them—as gaps. Then, by becoming aware of these interruptions in our dedication to the "other," our attention begins to fill these gaps with itself. The attention perceives its own absence, and in this perception attention meets itself. Discontinuity thus causes our I-consciousness to light up, on the plane on which our consciousness moves.

In pure thinking, the experience of evidence is identical with the act of cognition itself: the object and the cognizing are one. The given, the process in which it is given, and the concept all coincide.

When we read or perceive a text, the evidence lies in our understanding of the given signs in our reading, or "reading them together." When we read it, a text becomes obvious to us as text, regardless of the evidence of its contents.

The experience of evidence in perception is also a kind of reading. However, we have no concepts for these perceptual "textual signs," and therefore we do not even see them as signs. Instead of reading the signs, we measure and mathematize them and mistake their mathematical description for an understanding of them. The appropriate concepts rank higher than others and are more powerful; they are living, sentient, and willing concepts, which we encounter only in meditation.

The evidence of the perceptual world appears metamorphosed into the conviction that our percepts *exist*, that they are real. This is because we cannot think the perceptual world with our reflected dialectical consciousness, and therefore the part of perception that is not thought escapes the fate of finished thoughts. In other words, it does not fall onto the plane of the past but remains alive and active on the plane of the present during perception, thus giving it the character of reality. The true concepts of nature can be grasped only in meditation.

With the exception of technical and scientific terms, words do not have an unequivocal meaning; rather, a cloud of meanings surrounds them on the plane of thought. When we employ language merely as a vehicle to convey information, we use only a fraction of the cloud of meanings surrounding the words. For instance, the meaning of a word in a particular sentence is more or less unambiguously defined through the meaning of the sentence. The corresponding parts of their cloud of meanings then connect the words within the sentence.

Words are also surrounded by a cloud of *feeling*, which is shaped by the sound structure of the language concerned, above all by its vowels but also by the sound of the word as a whole. The cloud of meaning and the rhythm also contribute to the emotional character of words. Poets and writers in particular examine hard, soft, or airy words for their emotional value and use them accordingly. That is why we cannot express the meaning of a poem in terms of information. The cloud of feeling we are talking about here has nothing to do with any psychic "mood"; rather, it points to the sources of the conceptual meaning.

The original or *primal meaning* of words comprises the cloud of feelings as well as that of meanings. It belongs not so much to one particular word as to the words of a word group or word family that have a common or related root. Children grasp a word's original meaning when they hear the word used in a particular way and understand it. After that, they can understand and employ this word in all its known uses, and they can even discover new uses appropriate to it.

This means that when adults use a word in its specialized sense, the original, primal meaning resonates and covibrates with the specialized meaning, and children then experience it superconsciously. This continued presence of the primal meaning is particularly apparent in conjunctions and prepositions of Indo-European languages. In these languages we can see clearly how each sentence specifies and particularizes the original meaning, which is still present in the background. Indeed, we can use the same word in consecutive sentences, each time in a different sense.

The word that appears in the sensory world comes from the hidden, larger word, from the meaning of the particular sentence or sentences. If we train ourselves to experience this meaning consciously and without having to put it into words, we notice that the meaning in its living fluidity originates in an even more powerful word. The steps—the ladder of wordlike entities—by which the word descended until it became sense-perceptible can lead us gradually back up to *the* Word.[69]

The conscious experience of this "wordless word" is called meditation. This wordless word is not an abstraction; it is

---

69. See Kühlewind, *Das Licht des Wortes*, chapter "Die Himmelsleiter."

similar to such creative words as, for example, the ideas of natural phenomena.

In chapter 8 we showed that when we are dealing exclusively with thoughts and linguistic or textual phenomena, reality and truth coincide in the experience of evidence. In the sphere of perception, on the other hand, reality and truth are separated, because we cannot fully think through the percept if it is a part of nature; instead, we need higher concepts. Nevertheless, the outer image of nature, which has qualities and a lawfulness that can be described even without being read, leads us to the conclusion that we are dealing with a text. Wherever we discover differences and similarities, analogies and relations, we also find concepts, and wherever concepts appear in the perceptual world, we are dealing with a text.

The truths accessible to modern thinking become conscious when mirrored by our organism. As a result, these truths have lost their quality of reality. In contrast, the part of perception that is initially unthinkable remains alive—precisely because we cannot really think it—thus kindling the sensation of reality. As this part is active, the sensation of reality it evokes unites itself with the thinkable part of perception, that is, with the familiar nominal concepts. As a result, in thinking we have truth without reality, and in perception we have reality without truth.

Meditation is an attempt—by means of concentration and a continuity of attention in thinking and representing—to reach *a truth saturated with reality* in the experience of evidence. In perception on the other hand, that is to say, in perceptual meditation, the attempt is—again in the experience of evidence—to come to *a reality saturated with truth*. Meditation in any form always involves words. In fact, even the themes of pictorial and perceptual meditation are wordlike, although we cannot express such "words" in a particular language.

Meditation themes have been conceived with enhanced powers of cognition and are expressed in the form of a text or a picture. In perceptual meditation, we take our theme from nature; the phenomena of nature are in themselves expressions of higher concepts. The subjects we choose to meditate on do not describe facts or refer to a world that is already past. Rather, they point to the common source of world and cognition, that is, to the *Logos*. In the Logos all being is cognition and already contains the latter. We can cognize and know our outer and inner worlds because they are Logos worlds and are created through the Word. The text or theme we meditate on is taken from a phase of the way the word travels "downward" toward the world of the past and is then expressed in the words of a particular language or in a picture. For this reason a meditator can find the way up to the source of the theme through meditation— that is, we find the way into a "wordless" sphere, "wordless" if we define "word" as necessarily always having a sound.

"Word" implies structure also in a higher sense—the structure of a fluid, airy, warmthlike element. Because our ordinary language "structures" a much more dense and solid medium, when we meditate we have to develop a much more powerful faculty of structuring within our attention in order to be able to *cognize* at all in the thinner element. It is difficult to express higher experiences in the words or pictures of ordinary consciousness.[70]

However, we can overcome this difficulty if we resort to the primal meaning of words or to an archetype or symbol that is equally meaningful.

Meditation always lives in the sphere of evidence. There, truth and reality are one, reality and cognition are *one* being:

---

70. See Rudolf Steiner, *Kunst und Kunsterkenntnis* (GA 271) (Dornach, Switzerland: Rudolf Steiner Verlag, 1985), lectures of May 5 and 6, 1918.

the original, primeval word, not spoken, not audible, and not part of one particular language; it is the creative Word through which nature, our perceptual world, was created. In meditation we leave the plane of the past of our consciousness, then our theme becomes a task, which we can and must *realize*, so that the reality to be gained is at the same time truth, that is, evidence. We realize a text when we understand it, and we realize our I when our attention meets itself. Similarly, we create the reality of what we meditate on when our consciousness, now one with our theme, ascends to the corresponding level of the Word, the level from which our theme was taken.

10. Perceptual Meditation

....

To study the nature of a function of consciousness, it is well to examine its development, or its first occurrence, before it gets intermingled with habits, memories, and other mechanisms that distort the picture. Accordingly, to describe the activity of our senses in chapters 2 and 3, we had to go back to the directly given, that is, to the condition preceding the instruction of the senses by thought-intuitions—or at least to the beginning of this instruction. Now, however, we will look at the boundary of this instruction and at the conscious development of perception and thinking, whose interdependence we have already discussed in the above-mentioned chapters.

The middle senses (seeing and hearing) and the sense of touch provide everything for the higher senses—such as the I-sense (or you-sense), the sense of concepts, and the word sense—to understand. They provide the raw material for perception, which the higher senses then *read*, to the extent of their ability. In this reading, we always focus our attention on certain, selected features of the raw material while ignoring others. For instance, our word sense disregards the pitch of words to focus on their sound configuration; our thought sense concentrates on concepts and ignores words, and our "you-sense" forgets the thought content to focus only on the speaking I-being. In every case, the relatively lower senses are transparent and open to the relatively higher ones.

Conversation may be considered the archetype of perception. In conversation, we take in what our partner has said and break it up into sounds, words, thoughts, and I-cognition. Perhaps we hear the words but do not understand the other person's thoughts; in that case, we do not make use of the transparency of the word-sense. If we are unable to think what the other has said, the utterance will remain stuck on the level of the words. If we do not understand the language in which the utterance was made, what we heard remains only noise or, at most, sound. With this, our perception descends into the sphere of the middle senses. Our lower senses do not become transparent because the next higher functions above them are unable *to understand* what the lower senses convey.

Obviously, the natural world is not spoken in the here and now; rather, it is a finished text, much like a letter that was written in the past and must now be read. As long as we do not even know the individual letters of the text, much less the corresponding concepts and I-beings, nature remains for us a perception on the level of the middle senses and of the sense of touch. What happens when we do not understand our partner in conversation shows us that the middle senses convey unthinkable concepts to us, and do so superconsciously.

Perceptual meditation has the task of understanding the text of nature. To achieve this, we must raise our thinking to a more intuitive and living plane. Only then will our perceptual attention, now concentrated and trained to a heightened sensitivity for different qualities, be able to intuit the corresponding higher ideas. In other words, our thinking must not descend to the level of the past.

The text of nature does not consist of predetermined letters or signs whose meaning is clearly defined. *Discovering* these letters and signs is in itself a stage of meditation. All such acts of discovery constitute the finding of an understanding; they answer the question "What is to be perceived?" Just as we can "read" sounds in tones, words in sounds, and finally the thought content or meaning in words, so there is an act of "reading" involved in pure perceiving or perceptual meditation. If we cannot intuitively grasp the higher concepts we need, our perceiving remains on the level of the senses that have been appropriately instructed—after all, even the middle senses had to be instructed to be able to perceive the qualities they specifically focus on.

The more concentrated and the more unencumbered by concepts from the past our perceiving attention is, the more likely are we to be able to intuit the concepts of higher qualities in perception. In meditation we try to *distinguish* such concepts within the given we perceive. At the same time, we try to *integrate* these concepts into the perceptual picture that has come about as a result of their being distinguished within the given. In other words, in meditation we are trying to find *adequate* concepts. To find them, we must be on a higher plane of consciousness.

The presence of inadequate concepts makes it more difficult to reach such a higher level; therefore we must silence them. Intensifying and extending the phase of being given over to perception represents an attempt at silencing these inadequate concepts. When the quality and intensity of our perception are sufficiently enhanced, the concepts of the plane of the past— usually they are merely mental representations and not even concepts—can no longer interfere and disrupt it.

With our higher senses, we focus our attention on a world that exists only for human consciousness and that mirrors the inner structure of this consciousness. Since the higher senses, especially the sense of concepts, instruct all the other senses, our perceptual world is a specifically human one, as is also our world of thought.

As we ascend the series of the senses, the activities proper to the higher senses further individualize the raw material provided by the comparatively lower senses. For instance, a particular sentence is individualized by the I that utters it; it makes a difference *who* is saying it. This applies even on the level of mere information, where the reliability of the speaker and his or her particular point of view are important.

Every sentence, in turn, individualizes the words; of a word's many possible meanings, every sentence uses only a particular one—one that also often depends on the situation. If we disregard the speaker, the meaning of a sentence is less definite, and if we look at a word without considering the sentence of which it is a part, the meaning of the word is also less definite. Thus, the greater or more powerful wordlike entity becomes narrower, more defined, and more individualized as we ascend.

In comparison with the word, sound is the greater and more ambiguous wordlike entity. Within each word, several sounds narrow down each other's vast "meaning,"—which is unfathomable for our ordinary consciousness—to a smaller wordlike entity, namely, the word of which they are a part. For us, sounds are at the boundary of what we can grasp. Comprehension and concepts begin in the transition from sounds to words and continue in our understanding of sentences.

Perhaps in ancient times, by means of cognitive feeling, people understood words much more as sounds. Today, our understanding of words is very close to that of concepts. Because of the decadence of our languages, this relationship between sound and word is largely ruined.

Every sound forms within a tone, thus individualizing it. Tones, then, say more and are the greater idea of the two. However, people today hardly understand tones anymore—except perhaps in music and related arts. We still experience the sense-perceptible and the hidden part of words as symmetrically interrelated; but we have only a vague idea that the sounds of a particular language also have a hidden part, namely, their meaning. In contrast, we hardly experience tones as wordlike entities, and we have not the faintest idea what could complement sense-perceptible tones the way our comprehension complements the words we hear.

Our scarcity of names for different qualities of tones indicates that our conceptual consciousness is very far from grasping the true nature of tone. Most of the adjectives we use to describe tones, such as loud, low, deep, high (which could also be called differently), soft, hard, and so on, are borrowed from the other senses. Similarly, in the sphere of seeing, we have proper names for roughly eight colors. We have even fewer names for the perceptions of our senses of taste and of warmth. For the sense of smell, we have hardly anything more than "good smelling" and "bad smelling," that is, we really have no terms specific to these sense impressions.

Languages provide only scanty structure for the field of the middle senses, and this structure is rarely, if at all, based on their essential ideas. Nowadays our languages instruct us only in the ordinary concepts, and thus we can only instruct our senses in the same way. A true understanding of the sensory world requires the development of consciousness.

Perceptual meditation heightens our attention in the phase of being given over to the object of perception; that is, it enhances the activity of the I with which perception begins.[71]

---

71. See Steiner, *A Road to Self-Knowledge* (GA 16), chapter 1; *Anthroposophie: Ein Fragment,* Appendix 5; *The Being of Man and His Future Evolution* (GA 107) (London: Rudolf Steiner Press, 1981), lecture of December 8, 1908; *An Occult Physiology* (GA 128) (London: Rudolf Steiner Press, 1983), lecture of March 23, 1911; (GA 165), lecture of January 2, 1916; *Chance, Providence, and Necessity* (GA 163), lecture of August 30, 1915; (GA 205), lecture of July 16, 1921; (GA 206), lectures of August 12 and 13, 1921; *The Human Heart* (GA 212), lecture of May 26, 1922; (GA 218), lectures of October 20, 1922 and December 9, 1922; *Pastoral Medicine* (GA 318) (Hudson, N.Y.: Anthroposophic Press, 1987), lecture of September 10, 1924.

Without perceptual exercises we never become aware of our attention but only notice the results of its activity. For example, we see a mountain, but we are unaware of the "looking" attention that enables us to see it. The pictures we have in seeing and in other sensory perceptions are the results of our activity, of our attention; they are not memory pictures. These pictures are being woven in the immediate present, in the here-and-now, while we perceive. When we heighten the attention that is active in this process to the point where it can discover itself in its activity, then we will experience these pictures no longer as results but as the activity itself in all its liveliness. At the same time, the meaning of the meditation *"tat tvam asi,"* or "This is you," dawns on us.

The I lives in identity. Since the I initiates and guides even ordinary perception in giving itself over to the perceptual object, the perceptual picture is not subjective. We can verify this in conversation. We hear what our partner is saying, and then we can ascertain whether what we heard is identical with what was said. We can ask our partner in conversation about this, and he or she can confirm it. Indeed, normally we hear what was said—we do not expect anything else. We have no reason to assume that our relationship to "natural" perceptual elements differs from our relationship to another person's utterances in a conversation which can be verified.[72]

Thus, all pseudoproblems, such as whether different people experience the same sensory qualities, become less important. We cannot ascertain whether they do or not. Nor can we ascertain whether we ourselves always perceive the same sensory qualities. By this token, the pseudoconcept of "the same" is relativized.

---

72. See *Anthroposophie: Ein Fragment*, Appendix 5.

Other concepts fare similarly. We cannot define our basic concepts because that would require the existence of other, already-defined concepts, and so on. We understand each other in communication because we have an unshakable trust in the commonality of the word, even if this fact is the issue under discussion.

The directly given does not have a pregiven structure, neither a conceptual structure nor a perceptual one. After all, concepts isolate perceptions out of the given. Our sensory organs themselves structure the given only in cooperation with concepts—as the unique way each language subdivides the color spectrum proves.

When we have heightened the intensity of attention, we realize that this attention is identical with the picture it weaves. This leads to a monistic experience in pure perception. What is at work here is not human subjectivity; rather, it is the structuring, universal activity of wordlike attention—received from language, trained through conceptual thinking, and heightened by a schooling of consciousness. The new structuring of the given and the lighting up of higher concepts are one and the same act of consciousness. In and by such conscious activity we realize the ideal of Goethe's contemplative perception. At the same time, we rediscover in full consciousness the concepts that organically structure the given. In this type of meditation, the "text" and its elements remain ambiguous.

As we become aware of our attention as a creative reality, it lights up for us as the most intimate and individual activity of the I. When our I-experience occurs in perceptive attention, it reaches a level where the I becomes able to take in the language of natural phenomena. Then we discover that these phenomena have always been *speaking* to us, but we lacked the ability to understand this powerful language.

What natural phenomena are "saying" can be conveyed only in meditation sentences—if at all. The further we descend the ladder of the senses, down to the sense of smell, the more peace and harmony radiate toward us through a silence. This silence is also present in the tones and sounds of nature. It consists of the gaps between tones, and these gaps offer us the room to complement the phenomena. This silence is a waiting, in infinite patience and through immeasurable ages of peace that preceded any possibility of measurement.

We ourselves are the solution to the riddle of nature because we bear this solution within us, at least potentially. In particular, we have the ability to complement the sense-perceptible part of nature, enhancing it, so that it becomes reality. Of course, this is not the only and finite reality:

"In expectant sleep."
"Everything says: Peace."
"Unfathomable silence in the face of what is coming:
    Welcoming silence."
"Crumbling eternity."
"Beyond joy and sadness."
"Comes now the World-Light?"
"Are you prepared?"

If we do not elevate ourselves to the level of meditation, we will be blinded by the ideas of nature that exceed our comprehension. As these ideas are inaccessible to us, they implant themselves in our mind as perceptual sensations and make us believe that they contain a nonconceptual element. This nonconceptual element seems to affect our senses, but we could comprehend the ideal with our spirit. Our affected senses "respond," give us a picture. We assume that there is a non-ideal "reality-in-itself" behind this picture. However, in reality, these substitute concepts are merely mental pictures, impure "half-concepts," and lead us to misunderstand the nature of ideas. We mistake ideas for abstractions from the nonconceptual, as though concepts were not already a precondition for abstraction: after all, we must select and decide *what* we are abstracting *from*.

The systematic cultivation of "nonthoughts" leads to impenetrable inclusions in our consciousness that obstruct the healthy circulation of light. As a result, our intuitive thinking is more and more weakened. We construct a labyrinth made up of thoughts that move in circles, and we can hardly find a way out. The intuitive forces that are prevented from functioning in a healthy way then develop into the dynamic and powerful habits of our subconscious—into the inverted, yet profoundly effective, inspirations of our feeling and will. These work to prevent us from becoming truly human. Were they to succeed in this, nature would be eternalized in its obscured existence and unredeemed through our failure to read it with understanding—eternalized like a being that never wakes from its sleep, mummified while it sleeps.

In pure perception we are no longer blinded, and the incomprehensible regains its rank as a high idea. Our perception dissolves into understanding, into spiritual presence in the here and now.

Thus the human being realizes itself: becomes the meaning of the book of nature.

Epilogue

It is not the purpose of epistemology to make us conscious of what we are doing in any case, regardless of whether we are aware of it or not. To the extent epistemology does this, it is an *a posteriori* descriptive science, just as logic and linguistics are. Such description can at most serve as a preparation. The purpose of epistemology, rather, is to show that cognition is of a supersensible nature, that its nature is I-like. Moreover, epistemology leads us back to the *sources* of the given mode of cognition: from there, we can consciously continue our cognitive path for ourselves. In addition, epistemology also indicates where and how we can begin this continuation.

The kind of cognition that is given to us may be enhanced by conscious work. This is a new element in the evolution of humanity, particularly since such conscious development is not reserved for a few chosen people but is available for everybody.

Every stage of cognitive life has its own epistemology.[73] This must be given from a higher level through "insight" into the phase that is to be described—otherwise epistemology will end up as fruitless speculation. With insight from above, the description can be formed in such a way that we can understand it through thought-intuition, through the intuitive

---

73. See Kühlewind, *Stages of Consciousness*, chapter "The Two Stages of Consciousness."

formation of new concepts. This can be done even without first having to raise our consciousness to a new level. The intuitions needed for this prepare the conscious work needed to raise our cognitive life to a higher level.

Epistemology then serves as "study" for the cognitive path.[74]

That is why this book ends with chapters on meditation. These chapters were intended to show how a cognitive path, in the sense of spiritual science, can heal our unhealthy cognizing and develop it organically. This path, given to us as a possibility, is a heightening of cognition.

---

74. See Kühlewind, *The Life of the Soul*, chapters 3 and 5.

Bibliographical References

Books by Rudolf Steiner:

Anthroposophical Leading Thoughts (GA 26). London: Rudolf Steiner Press, 1973.
Anthroposophy and the Inner Life (GA 234). Suffolk, England: Rudolf Steiner Press, 1992.
The Being of Man and His Future Evolution (GA 107). London: Rudolf Steiner Press, 1981.
The Boundaries of Natural Science (GA 322). Hudson, N.Y.: Anthroposophic Press, 1983. (GA 322).
The Case for Anthroposophy (GA 21). London: Rudolf Steiner Press, 1970.
Chance, Providence, and Necessity (GA 163). Hudson, N.Y.: Anthroposophic Press, 1988.
The Effects of Spiritual Development (GA 145). London: Rudolf Steiner Press, 1978.
Foundations of Esotericism (GA 93a). London: Rudolf Steiner Press, 1982.
Fruits of Anthroposophy. Hudson, N.Y.: Anthroposophic Press, 1986.
Goethean Science (GA 1), previously translated as *Goethe the Scientist.* Spring Valley, N.Y.: Mercury Press, 1988.
Goethe's World View (GA 6). Spring Valley, N.Y.: Mercury Press, 1985.
How Do I Find the Christ (GA 182). Hudson, N.Y.: Anthroposophic Press, 1941.
The Human Heart (GA 212). Spring Valley, N.Y.: Mercury Press, 1985.
Knowledge and Initiation (GA 211). Vancouver, B.C.: Steiner Book Centre, n.d.
Macrocosm and Microcosm, (GA 119). London: Rudolf Steiner Press, 1968.
Metamorphoses of the Soul, vol. 1 (GA 59). London, Rudolf Steiner Press, 1983.
The Michael Mystery (GA 26). Spring Valley, N.Y.: St. George Publications, 1984.
The Mission of the Archangel Michael (GA 194). Spring Valley, N.Y.: Anthroposophic Press, 1961.
A Modern Art of Education (GA 307). Hudson, N.Y.: Anthroposophic Press, 1972.
An Occult Physiology (GA 128). London: Rudolf Steiner Press, 1983.
An Outline of Occult Science (GA 13). Hudson, N.Y.: Anthroposophic Press, 1989.

Pastoral Medicine (GA 318). Hudson, N.Y.: Anthroposophic Press, 1987.

The Philosophy of Freedom (GA 4). Hudson, N.Y.: Anthroposophic Press, 1986.

The Riddle of Humanity (GA 170). London: Rudolf Steiner Press, 1990.

The Riddle of Man (GA 20). Spring Valley, N.Y.: Mercury Press, 1990.

A Road to Self-Knowledge (GA 16). London: Rudolf Steiner Press, 1975.

Spiritual Science as a Foundation for Social Forms (GA 199). Hudson, N.Y.: Anthroposophic Press, 1986.

Study of Man. London; Rudolf Steiner Press, 1966.

A Theory of Knowledge (GA 2). Hudson, N.Y.: Anthroposophic Press, 1978.

Three Streams in Human Evolution (GA 184). London: Rudolf Steiner Press, 1965.

Truth and Knowledge (GA 3). Blauvelt, N.Y.: Rudolf Steiner Publications, 1981.

The World of the Senses and the World of the Spirit (GA 134). Spring Valley, N.Y.:Anthroposophic Press, 1979.

Books by Georg Kühlewind:

Becoming Aware of the Logos. Hudson, N.Y.: Lindisfarne Press, 1985.

Das Licht des Wortes ("Light of the Word"). Stuttgart: Verlag Freies Geistesleben,1984.

Der Sprechende Mensch ("The Speaking Human Being"). Frankfurt: Vittorio Klostermann, 1992.

Die Diener des Logos ("Servants of the Logos"). Stuttgart: Verlag Freies Geistesleben,1981.

Die Wahrheit Tun ("Doing the Truth"). Stuttgart: Verlag Freies Geistesleben, 1978.

The Life of the Soul. Hudson, N.Y.: Lindisfarne Press, 1990; [*Das Leben der Seele*]. Stuttgart: Verlag Freies Geistesleben, 1982.

Schooling of Consciousness. Fair Oaks, California: Rudolf Steiner College Publications, 1985.

Stages of Consciousness. Hudson, N.Y.: Lindisfarne Press, 1984.

Books by other Authors:

Berger, P.L. *A Rumor of Angels.* New York: Bantam, Doubleday, Dell, Anchor Books, 1981.

König, Karl. *Sinnesentwicklung und Leibeserfahrung.* Stuttgart: Verlag Freies Geistesleben, 1978.

Scaligero, Massimo. *Segreti del Tempo e del Spazio.* Rome: Tilopa, 1964.